It's Simple to Live the Life of Your Dreams

Success Made Simple

Life
and the
Law of Motion

by Michael Weston

THE OFFICIAL USER'S MANUAL FOR YOUR LIFE

BALBOA.
PRESS
A DIVISION OF HAY HOUSE

Balboa Press books may be ordered through booksellers or by contacting:

Balboa Press
A Division of Hay House
1663 Liberty Drive
Bloomington, IN 47403
www.balboapress.com.au
1-(877) 407-4847

ISBN: 978-1-4525-1155-9 (sc)
ISBN: 978-1-4525-1156-6 (e)

Because of the dynamic nature of the Internet, any web addresses or links contained in this book may have changed since publication and may no longer be valid. The views expressed in this work are solely those of the author and do not necessarily reflect the views of the publisher, and the publisher hereby disclaims any responsibility for them.

The author of this book does not dispense medical advice or prescribe the use of any technique as a form of treatment for physical, emotional, or medical problems without the advice of a physician, either directly or indirectly. The intent of the author is only to offer information of a general nature to help you in your quest for emotional and spiritual well-being In the event you use any of the information in this book for yourself, which is your constitutional right, the author and the publisher assume no responsibility for your actions.

Balboa Press rev. date: 09/28/2013

*To my daughter: what I understand now,
that I wish I knew in my 20's.*

Contents

Introduction

"You cannot teach a man anything; you can
only help him find it within himself."
—Galileo

Most books today are written to entertain. The purpose of this book is to enlighten. This book gives you the opportunity to take control of your life, to understand how life works, and to use that understanding to get what you want out of life.

Over the years, I've been fortunate enough to meet a lot of successful people. The thing that strikes me about them is that they are all very different. They come from a wide variety of backgrounds. Some were young and others "not so young." Some had rich parents, and some had poor. Some are highly educated, and some never finished high school. Some are flamboyant and outgoing, and others are so quiet and reserved that you would hardly know they're there.

What each of these successful people have in common is an understanding of how life works. They understand the handful of basic principles that lead to a successful life. These principles are not a secret. They are there for anyone who chooses to seek them out. By reading this book, you too will learn the principles required to live a successful life and some simple techniques to put those principles to work in your life.

If you are like most of us, some things in life are going your way, and some things aren't. There are also times when everything seems to go your way and other times where nothing seems to go right. Welcome to life.

Your life will never be perfect, because there is no such thing as perfection. Successful people understand that there can only ever be continuous improvement in the areas that matter to them. By the time you've finished reading this book, you'll understand why this is so and how you can take back control and get on the road to a new life of continuous improvement.

In order for you to succeed at whatever it is you want to achieve in life, you have to understand how life works. You have to understand how you move towards what you want and how you move away from what you don't want. It's an unfortunate fact that most people will go through life and have no understanding as to why their life turns out as it does. Invariably, they blame other people, their teachers, their boss, the government, society, the world, and sometimes even life itself. The last place people look when things go wrong is in the mirror. Successful people understand that they are the masters of their destiny. This book will give you the tools necessary to become the master of your destiny.

Throughout this book, we will talk about success, so it's important to agree on what we mean by success. When you talk about success, most people will immediately think you're talking about financial success. It's important to remember that while we make a living from what we receive, we make a life from what we give.

Success will look different for each of us. Your picture of what success looks like will be different from mine. If success looked the same for all of us, we'd all have the same friends, work in the same job, live in the same house, drive the same car, wear the same clothes, and so on and so on. In other words, the world would be a very boring place. You must be the one who decides what constitutes a successful life. You must be the one who makes the decisions and takes the required actions, because you will be the one who will be living that life. No one should tell you what kind of life you should live any more than the telephone should tell you what you should say. As we progress, you will be given the process to determine your definition of success and the tools to start moving towards that definition.

I've always been amazed by those who see themselves as unsuccessful or believe that success in life is only available to others and is virtually unobtainable for themselves. Invariably, these same people equate success solely to great financial achievements. While no one would argue that financial factors play a role in your sense of wellbeing, it is not the only thing that matters, and arguably it is one of the least important in your quest for true success. Study after study, conducted in numerous countries and across a variety of cultures, has consistently shown that once your basic financial requirements have been met (e.g., food, shelter, clothing, etc.), the ability of additional money to increase your sense of wellbeing falls dramatically.

True success is about achieving prosperity, not just wealth. Prosperity goes well beyond financial outcomes alone. A prosperous life involves good health, enriching relationships, engaging occupations, and adhering to the values you believe are important. No one in his or her right mind would consciously trade any of the above for some more money. Ask yourself whether you'd trade your family, your health, or your values for more money. I doubt you would. Nor would anyone else. In order to be truly successful and achieve a lasting sense of wellbeing, happiness, and contentment, you have to seek prosperity, not wealth. To be prosperous is to truly thrive. Therefore, in order to live a prosperous life, you must be successful in each of the five key areas of your life. In this sense, prosperity is simply being able to spend your life living as you desire.

I decided to write this book because I felt it needed to be written. After a lifetime of study, practical experience, successes, and failures, I thought to myself, "What do I wish someone had told me when I first started out on this journey through life?" This book is the result. Through this book, I will try to distil principles that have been studied and taught for thousands of years by philosophers, religious leaders, and educators into a simple, usable framework that each of us will be able to apply in our daily lives. These principles work for anyone who wishes to learn them and apply them.

Think of this book as the user's manual for your life. We're given a user's manual for just about everything of significance that we own. However, we've never been given a user's manual for the most important thing we own: our lives. I was never taught any of the principles in this book throughout my eighteen years of formal education. I was able to learn them only through years of trial and error, independent study, and both good and bad experiences. Now I pass them on to you.

User's manuals are short and concise. They give you the important information in a simple, usable format. They don't provide you with useless or seldom used information. They don't use big words to sound impressive. They give you what you need to make it work for you, and that's all. So, this book is purposely short. There is no use in saying that success is simple and then taking five hundred pages explaining how simple it is. Achieving success is simple, once you understand how it works, and the principles outlined in this book can be readily understood and implemented by anyone who decides to do it.

"It is a simple task to make things complex, but
a complex task to make them simple."
—Meyer's Law

It's a constant challenge to get people to understand what you mean when you say that becoming a success in life is simple. When you say simple, people immediately think you mean easy. Believe me, simple and easy are not the same thing. If becoming successful in life were easy, everyone would be successful. Being successful in life is not easy, but it is simple.

As an example, doing a single push-up is both simple and easy. You assume a plank position with your arms fully extended. Then you bend your arms until your chin touches the ground. Then you straighten your arms to return to the starting position. See, both simple and easy. However, doing fifty push-ups, while still simple, is no longer easy. You see, the word "simple" relates to the complexity of the task. How hard is it for someone to understand what it is they should do? The complexity in doing a push-up is the same for the first push-up as it is for the fiftieth. However, the word "easy" relates to the degree of difficulty, whether physical or mental, in taking the action required to complete or continue the task. Obviously, it is far more difficult to do the fiftieth push-up than it was to do the first. So, success is simple, not easy.

I write as I speak—simply, honestly, and directly. I want you to clearly understand the principles explained here, and I want to make sure they are readily useable by anyone who cares to follow those principles. My intention is never to upset or offend anyone, but if for some reason I do, I apologize in advance. I hope that everyone will remember that the message is far more important than the messenger.

This book will provide you with a step-by-step process to get clarity about what's important to you and what you want to achieve in each area of your life. It takes setting aside some time to focus on your life, putting some thought into what you believe to be important, and thinking about what you actually want to achieve from life. The activities in Part 3 of this book will help you do this. It's a fairly simple process, although it does require you to devote the necessary time to truly think about the sorts of things that most of us never really spend any time thinking about. Applying the principles you will learn in this book, day in and day out, is where the challenge begins.

"The step from knowing to doing is rarely taken."
—Ralph Waldo Emerson

There is a difference between knowing the path and walking the path. By the time you have finished this book, you will know the path to success, and you will see how simple it is. This book will show you the path, but you are the one who must walk it.

Enjoy the Journey!

PART 1

How Life Works

Part 1 of this book will deal with the basic facts about how life works. I am not proposing some new theory. It is just how it is. The way life works has been the same for thousands of years. Our understanding of these facts has been aided by the input from generations upon generations of people from all walks of life. You may not like the fact that the sun rises in the east, but it doesn't change the fact that it does. You may wish to think that life works differently now than in the past, but it doesn't. You must understand these "facts of life" in order to use them to your best advantage.

CHAPTER 1

The Law of Motion

"A body at rest tends to stay at rest. A body in motion tends to stay in motion, at the same speed and in the same direction, unless acted upon by another force."
—Sir Isaac Newton

The law of motion is what's known as a natural law. A natural law is defined as "a theory that posits the existence of laws whose contents are set by nature and are valid in all things." A common example of a natural law is the law of gravity, which was also attributed to Sir Isaac Newton (1642-1727). If any of you jumped out of a tree or off a ladder while thinking you could fly, as I did when I was young, you quickly learned that the law of gravity applied to you as it did to everyone and everything else. No matter how hard you flapped your arms, you still fell like a stone. There is no escaping a natural law.

Examples of motion are everywhere in the natural world. Aristotle (384-322 BC) tried to determine the causes of motion—what made things move—without any real success. However, Galileo (1564-1642) turned the scientific thinking on motion around by proposing that, rather than focusing on *why* things moved, scientists should work on discovering *how* things moved. As a result, a whole new philosophy of physics was created.

Sir Isaac Newton was born the year Galileo died. Sir Isaac Newton's work in the 1680s produced a nearly perfect answer to Galileo's proposal for investigation when Newton posited the law of motion. The law of motion, as it is known, is one such "natural law," and it applies as equally to the movement of planets around the sun as it does to the trajectory of a ball you might roll along the floor. In other words, natural laws apply equally to all things. That includes us.

Inertia

> "If you think the way you've always thought, then
> you'll do the things you've always done and
> keep getting what you've always gotten."
> —Unknown

The first part of Newton's law of motion relates to inertia. Inertia is the resistance of an object to a change in its state of motion. For example, if you place a ball in the middle of a flat, even floor, it will remain there. It won't roll off or just fly away. If you roll it, all things being equal, it will tend to roll in a straight line.

If you apply the principle of inertia to people, it means that we are likely to continue doing whatever it is that we have been doing. Inertia is what keeps us doing the same things the same way that we have always done them. You might also call them habits of behaviour. If what you have been doing in your life has been serving you well and is taking you where you want to go, then inertia is your friend. If parts of your life have not been going the way that you want them to, then inertia is something you must struggle against. Inertia is your natural resistance to change your habits of behaviour. Habits are simply well-worn ways of thinking.

Change is not something that comes easily for most people. In fact, many people will go to great lengths to avoid having to make changes in their lives. We all fear change to one degree or another. Have you ever been to a class, a meeting, or a seminar that has carried on over a number of sessions? Have you noticed how, after each break, people always seem to return to the same seat? That is inertia in action. For many people, even changing seats presents a real mental challenge. Try sitting in a seat that was previously occupied by someone else and watch the person's reaction. Even small changes are not easy, but the ability to make changes is an absolute necessity if you're going to improve any aspect of your life.

Motion

All things on this planet are in motion at all times. Our planet is hurtling around the sun at about 110,000 kilometres per hour (68,000 mph). Within the temperate zone, the earth is spinning on its axis at about 1,000 to 1,700 kph (620 to 1,060 mph). Like it or not, everyone and everything is in motion all the time.

> "The best thing about the future is that
> it comes one day at a time."
> —Abraham Lincoln

We are also constantly moving through time. An average life consists of about 30,000 days. That is the average number of days between the day we are born and the day we die. That's about 720,000 hours. If we subtract the average number of hours spent sleeping, we are left with about 480,000 waking hours to build this thing we call life. If you are reading this, you have probably already used up a large percentage of those hours.

What each of us needs to remember is that we experienced an incredible amount of good luck simply by being born. No one can legitimately say he or she has never been lucky because we all effectively won the lottery at birth. Out of the millions of possible genetic combinations that could have occurred at conception, we were the lucky ones. Yes, at birth, we may not all be equal in the attributes that a fickle society has chosen to value at this point in time, but we do all have an average of 30,000 days given to us. We each have a combination of characteristics, skills, and abilities that are unique to us. Like snowflakes, there is no one else in the world exactly like us. As a result, each of our lives will be unique too. It is up to each of us, as unique individuals, to determine what attributes we decide are important to us and what things we should strive for.

Speed and Direction

The second part of the law of motion has to do with speed and direction. If you roll a ball along the floor, you can roll it fast or slow. You can also roll it in any direction you desire. However, once the ball leaves your hand, it will be at the speed and in the direction that you rolled it.

In life, we're each moving at a given speed and in a certain direction. Simply stated, as we move through life, we must be moving in a direction. Movement requires a direction, and that direction is either *towards* the things we want in life or *away* from the things we want. The speed at which we are moving is determined by the decisions we make and the actions we take.

Given that this is occurring, whether we like it or not, it is important that we understand and accept it and that we learn to exert control over as much of it as possible so that we are going in the direction and at the speed we desire.

Other Forces

The final part of the law of motion relates to the "other forces" that can change both the speed and the direction of an object. If you roll a ball along the floor, it won't continue to roll indefinitely. The law of gravity will keep the ball on the floor, which will create friction. That friction will slow the ball down over time. For example, the ball will roll farther on tiles than on carpet because there is less friction on tiles. Wind can change the direction of the ball. If the ball hits a wall, the impact will cause the ball to lose speed and change direction.

Once that ball leaves your hand, it is out of your control and is subject to a host of other forces that will impact its journey.

Our personal journeys through life are also influenced by a host of other forces. These forces fall into two primary groups. There are those things in life over which we have no control, and there are those over which we do have control. Even though we can't control everything that happens to us in life, we can control our reactions to the things that happen. This gives us the ability to capitalize on the good things that happen unexpectedly and to mitigate the negative impact from the bad things that happen.

"Remembering you are going to die is the best way I know to avoid the trap of thinking you have something to lose."
—Steve Jobs, Apple CEO, 2005 Stanford University address

Here is the unvarnished truth: you can't get out of life alive. It's that simple. No one is going to achieve the things they want to achieve in life once their time is up. Unless you believe in reincarnation, you're not coming back. This is a one-way trip. There is no second chance. Therefore, it makes no sense at all *not* to pursue the things that are important to you in life, and you should do it now. You have been given the precious gift of life. Don't waste it. This is your one shot to make a difference in the world. Steve Jobs said he wanted "to make a ding in the universe." I don't think anyone could reasonably argue that he didn't do just that. You too have the ability to make your mark in the world.

Unfortunately, I think the reason most people don't make their mark is that they really haven't thought about, decided on, and committed to whatever that mark is. It doesn't need to be some grandiose plan. It may be as simple as raising your children to be the best people they can possibly be. It may be to become the best friend anyone would ever hope to have. The important thing is not what kind of mark you choose to make in the world, but that you thought about it, chose it, and then made it happen. When you were born, you were given about 30,000 days, so do something special with them.

Don't drift through life in the grey haze of getting through the day, week, month, etc. Decide what you're going to do in this life, and then get out there and make it happen. The only chance you have to make your mark is between now and the end of your 30,000 days. Don't count the days; make the days count. No one achieves his or her goals in the graveyard, except the Undertaker.

None of this is meant to frighten or depress you; it is meant to make you think about where you are in life, right now, and the direction in which your life is heading. It is also meant to create a sense of urgency in doing what's necessary to get moving in the "right" direction. The direction you consciously choose. Make today the beginning of your new "journey to making a difference." Start now and don't let anyone or anything get in your way. It's your life, no one else's. While we may share our lives with others, at the end of our days, we each go into the pine box alone. Last I heard, they still have a "one-to-a-box" rule.

Why is taking stock of where we are in life important? As with any journey, it is important to know the starting point. If we don't know where we are, we don't know what we need to do to move towards what we want in life. Regardless of whether you're happily aware or painfully aware of where you are in life, it is vital that each of us is honest with ourselves, as we go through this book, in order to maximize the benefits from reading it.

CHAPTER 2

Motion

"Time is the coin of your life. It is the only coin you have,
and only you can determine how it will be spent. Be
careful lest you let other people spend it for you."
—Carl Sandburg

Every one of us was born rich. The most valuable assets we
have are not our houses, our cars, our investments, or our bank
accounts. The most precious thing known to man . . . is time. The
most valuable asset we have is life.

Time is the one asset that both rich and poor are born with.
Time isn't dependent upon wealth, intelligence, beauty, physical
prowess, or any of the attributes society tends to use to establish
the relative "success" of an individual. Time is given freely to
each of us. You can spend it on your family, your friends, your
health, your finances, the TV, the Internet, or whatever else you
choose. You can invest it wisely—or you can waste it foolishly.
What you do with your time is up to you. A prosperous life is about
striving to improve the quality of that time.

Prosperity isn't about having a flashy house and a great car, if
it means you sacrifice your health and lose touch with the people
you care about to get them. It's not a good trade to have lots
of money if you are doing something you hate because it goes

against the values you hold dear. Living a prosperous life is not about sacrificing one part of your life to subsidize another. Time is the currency of your life. We must each spend that currency wisely.

Too often, we allow ourselves to get side-tracked by urgent things we must do now, so that we never seem to get around to doing the important things we need to do to build the life we want. "I'll do it tomorrow" is a phrase repeated often by many of us. The problem with "tomorrow" is that it never comes. When tomorrow gets here, we call it today. In fact, today is yesterday's tomorrow, and as each tomorrow arrives, another of our 30,000 days has slipped through our fingers. Too many of us wasted yesterday, are wasting today, and will likely waste tomorrow too.

Each day, we must ask ourselves, "What did I accomplish with the opportunity that today provided me? What did I do today to move myself towards the life I aspire to lead?" If we don't stay focused on the important things in life, we will inevitably discover that the life that might have been will have slipped through our hands, one "tomorrow" at a time.

It is critical to your success that you understand and accept that you are moving unstoppably through life. You have no choice in this. Each day that passes is one more of the 30,000 days that make up your life that's been spent. By the time you reach the age of twenty-one, you will have used up about 25 per cent of those days. By the age of forty, you have used almost 50 per cent of your available days. At sixty, almost 75 per cent of your days will be behind you.

That said, the opposite is also true. At twenty-one, you have 75 per cent of your life to look forward to. At forty, you're still not halfway there, and at sixty you still have more than 25 per cent of your life ahead of you. No matter how old you are today, you have all the time you need to do the important things. Most of us will have tomorrow, another week, another month, and even another year. In fact, most of us have several decades left in our lives. We have all the time we need to live the life we choose to lead.

> "Most people over-estimate what they can accomplish in a year and under-estimate what they can accomplish in a decade."
> —Anthony Robbins

We still have lots of time and a wealth of opportunity to show the world what we can do. However, we can just as easily let our tomorrows slip by, just as we let our yesterdays slip by. We don't have an endless supply of days. To achieve success in any area of your life, you must be able to spot opportunities quickly, make fast decisions, and take action immediately. You must live your life with a sense of urgency. If you're going to stand, stand; if you're going to move, move; but don't just wobble. Opportunities come to all of us, but opportunity is like a snowflake that sparkles brilliantly in your hand for only a moment before it melts away. You must be ready to move when the next opportunity presents itself, because you never know when it will happen next.

While we each start off with an average 30,000 days, it's important to remember that that is just an average. Some things we can't change. Hereditary factors can lengthen or shorten it, but that's still the average. Some things you can change. If you eat junk food, get overweight, smoke, drink too much or engage in other high-risk activities, you can shorten it. If you stay fit, eat well and avoid doing the things you know you shouldn't do, you can lengthen it. Either way, it's up to you.

We'll use about 25 per cent of our lives getting through school and preparing for what lies ahead. We'll use almost another 25 per cent of our lives getting from retirement to the finish line. That means that we have just over 50 per cent of our lives, or 240,000 waking hours, within which we will build our careers, our families, and most of what we will look back on as *life*.

One of the principles propounded in the *Tao Te Ching* is that we can only go one of two directions in life. We can either move towards what we want or away from what we want. If you think about it, you begin to realize the importance of that principle. There is no middle ground. If you are not moving towards what you want in life, than any other direction you go, is the wrong direction.

Since everyone seems to focus on it, lets take, for example, money. You're either saving it or spending it. There is nothing else you can do with it. You're doing one of those two things with every dollar you get. Is your current proportion of saving to spending moving you toward, or away from, your financial goals? If you want to lose weight, it's a simple matter of "input" and "output." How many calories are you "putting in" your mouth versus how many calories are you burning up by "putting out" effort?

You will find that most things in life are binary. They are the opposite sides of the same coin. Save money /spend money; gain weight/lose weight; make friends/lose friends; joy/despair; summer/winter; sunshine/rain and on and on. Life is made up of both sides of each coin. You can't have one side of the coin without the other. In most cases, you wouldn't even recognize one side of the coin without having experienced the other. For example, you would not know what being warm was like, unless you have also experienced being cold.

That's why it's so important for each of us to have complete clarity about what we want from our lives. If we don't know exactly what we want, how will we know if we're moving towards it or away from it? This life is not a dress rehearsal; it's the real thing. We have each been given one lifetime to accomplish what we choose to accomplish. No one can do everything, but everyone can do something.

> "Do or do not; there is no try."
> Yoda, *Star Wars*

We must each determine, for ourselves, what we will work towards achieving in our lives and then set about doing it. Life provides no room to "try" to do something. Don't hedge your bets. You must decide what is important to you in your life and then start moving towards it. You must stay focused on your destination. Continually check your progress and re-adjust your direction if you find you're drifting off course.

You must ask yourself constantly, is this thing I'm about to do going to get me closer to where I want to be? If it isn't, then don't do it. We live in a country that provides each of us with ample opportunity to strive for what we want in life and a safety net to catch us if we fall. That's an advantage that the vast majority of people in the world don't have. Why do you think so many people are trying so hard to get into this country? It's because we truly do live in a land of opportunity and there really is no excuse for us not to go after what we want out of life.

How have you spent your time so far? Would you say you've invested your "life's capital" wisely? How much "life capital" do you have left to spend? What do you intend to spend it on? Your "life capital" is a declining resource. Each day that passes means that you have less of it than you did the day before. If you really want to know what you truly value in life, what you really believe to be important, then look at where you spend your time. What are you saying if you spend more time watching TV, or on the Internet, than you spend with your family or your friends? What are you saying if you spend more time using Social Media, then you do staying fit? If you want to be honest, instead of saying, "I haven't got the time," you should say, "It's really not that important to me." We all have the same amount of time each day. You will never have more time. You have all the time you will ever have right now. It's not about the time; it's about how you choose to spend it.

"Until you value your self, you won't value your time.
Until you value your time, you will not do anything with it."
—M. Scott Peck

How you spend your time says more, about the things that are important to you, than what you say is important to you. If you want to know what people truly value, in their life, look at what they do, not what they say. Success comes from what you do, not what you say. In other words, don't waste your time telling people what's important to you, because you show them every day by what you do. We may judge ourselves by our intent, but others judge us by our actions. What action have you taken today to create the life you want?

You come into this world with no hair, no teeth and no money. Like it or not you're probably going out the same way. There is no use in getting to the end of your life having achieved little of what you had hoped for, because you chose to take it easy and play it safe. Better you slide sideways into that final resting place of life screaming, "What a ride!"

CHAPTER 3

Direction

"You have brains in your head. You have feet in your shoes. You can steer yourself any direction you choose. You're on your own. And you know what you know.
And *you* are the one who'll decide where to go."
—Dr Seuss, *Oh, The Places You'll Go!*

There are five key directions in which each of us is heading in life. These are the five key areas of life by which we will determine whether we believe our lives to be a success or not. The previous chapter explained how we are all moving, all the time. If we are moving, we must be moving in a direction. That direction is either towards or away from the things we want to achieve in life. There are five key areas of life, within which all the major elements of our lives reside.

These five areas are:

- relational
- occupational
- financial
- physical
- philosophical

The *relational* area of life has to do with the wide variety of relationships we have with different people. By definition, relational means the way in which two or more people are connected. We have different types of relationships, depending on whether the people involved are partners, family, friends, co-workers, people in our communities, or others we regularly come in contact with. The relational part of life is the social element of our lives. It is about the people we choose to spend time with.

The direction of our lives can be measured by the quality of our relationships with the significant people in our lives. Ask yourself how you feel about your significant relationships. Compare your feelings about them now versus a year ago. Do you think the relationship is improving? For example, how is your relationship going with your partner? What about your best friend or your work-mates? Are these relationships better now than they were a year ago? Do you feel they're getting better? Stronger? We must regularly take the temperature of our relationships to make sure that we don't take one of the most important areas of life for granted.

An old adage says, "On your deathbed, no one ever wishes they'd spent more time at the office." As humans, we are tribal by nature. We have an innate need to belong to something that gives meaning to our lives. We yearn to be a part of something beyond ourselves. Our partners, families, friends, co-workers, and communities fill a vital role in giving meaning to our lives. Too often, we neglect this vital part of our lives as we struggle to cope with an increasingly busy life. We will never feel happy and successful unless we have the balance right in the relational part of our lives.

The *occupational* part of life has to do with the activities we use to occupy our time. This includes our work or studies—and how we spend time outside of normal working or school hours (our hobbies, what we read, the sports we play, the TV we watch, and the time we spend on the Internet or playing games). We all have a desire to achieve, to improve, and to grow. This desire is often fulfilled through the intellectual challenge of our work or studies, but this sense of fulfilment may also come from improving our skills through other pursuits. The occupational part of life is about what we spend our lives doing.

The *financial* area of life has to do with an individual's sense of financial well-being. This is not merely about achieving financial independence—it is about establishing a sense of financial security. This has to do with the degree of freedom from worry that we have in regards to our financial affairs. The financial area of life is about the quality of life we live.

Most of us have this idea about what would make us feel financially secure, but we've never really calculated the cost. Have you ever really priced the house, the car, and the personal belongings in this "real-world" life? I'm not talking about some fantasy life you imagine living after you win the lottery, but the real, down-to-earth lifestyle that you're willing to work for to achieve. Many people are very surprised to learn that their "real-world" life isn't as expensive as they imagined. I'm not saying that you shouldn't strive to live an aspirational lifestyle, but once you've conquered your "real-world" requirements, you can focus on moving towards your "ideal" lifestyle. There is often a very big financial gap between what you really need to be happy and secure financially and what you might like to have in an "ideal" world. That's what moving in a direction is all about. Think of "secure" as a milestone on your way to "ideal".

Unfortunately, the financial area of life is the one that tends to get the greatest focus. Many people falsely believe that they need a great deal of money to get this part of their life right—and they can't be happy until they do. Nothing could be further from the truth. An extra million dollars may relieve some short-term financial stress, but it will not make you happy. Study after study, in different countries and cultures, has shown that once our financial resources are sufficient to take care of our basic survival and security needs, more money adds little to the level of a person's sense of happiness. If you understand Abraham Maslow's Hierarchy of Needs, this makes perfect sense.

Maslow's research in psychology and human motivation postulated a hierarchical pyramid structure to the priority we place in fulfilling our human needs. His pyramid started with basic human survival and security needs at the bottom and things like love, friendship, self-esteem, and personal growth at the top. Simply put, this is why the financial part of life has been shown to have little impact on our levels of happiness after we have achieved sufficient monetary resources to meet our survival and security needs.

> "Of the billionaires I have known, money just brings out
> the basic traits in them. If they were jerks before they had
> money, they are simply jerks with a billion dollars now."
> —Warren Buffett

Your financial position does little to enhance your higher level *needs*, such as love, friendship, self-esteem, and personal growth. These higher-level human needs are what ultimately create happiness once your basic survival and security needs have been covered. There is truth to the old saying that money can't buy happiness. While it is important that we get the financial area of life right, we must understand that it is not the most important area of life and is not the one that will ultimately make us happy.

The *physical* area of life relates to a person's quality of health. Good health is vital to an individual's sense of well-being and happiness. We've all had a bad cold or the flu at some point in life. While you were ill, did you feel like doing anything? Of course not—because ill health unavoidably impacts every other area of life. Illness should be a reminder to each of us of just how important health is and that good health is critical to overall happiness. The physical area of life is about how we live.

Too often, people sacrifice health in the pursuit of more money. Long hours, stress, lack of exercise, smoking, and poor eating habits are often the consequences of the single-minded pursuit of money. While their effects might not be immediately apparent, poor lifestyle choices take a toll on people's health every year. Interestingly, if you asked these same people if they would trade their health for more money, they would say definitely not—yet they continue to abuse their bodies on a daily basis.

The human body is a miraculous machine. However, this "miraculousness," like most things in life, is a two-sided coin. It is a blessing and a curse. It is a blessing because if you change your lifestyle choices, your body has the ability to begin healing itself. Smokers' lungs can begin to clear if no permanent damage has been done. Blood pressure and blood sugar issues can often begin to correct themselves when an obese person loses the extra weight. The human body can work to repair myriad health issues if we just give it a chance by helping it out. However, this same miraculous healing ability is also a curse because it allows many people to think they are getting away with poor choices—when they really aren't. If you abuse your health long enough, your actions will eventually win out, your body will give up, and you'll become ill.

Obesity is one of the biggest health issues facing modern society. Fad diets, crash diets, hyper-restrictive diets, and a host of other purported quick fixes have proven to be ineffective. The fact is that no one became overweight overnight. Fat doesn't just show up magically one morning. It accumulates slowly, over time. Getting fat is the result of thousands of poor decisions made over a long period of time. If it was okay to allow it to accumulate over time, why do we think it must instantly disappear? Past lifestyle choices put it on, and future lifestyle choices can take it off. Going on a crash program only to return to the same lifestyle choices, which put the weight on in the first place, is a recipe for failure and disappointment. Subtle lifestyle changes and food choices that you can make a permanent part of your life are the best ways to make a permanent change. It may take longer to get the weight off in the first place, but your new lifestyle will ensure that it stays off.

The same basic principles outlined above can work wonders on a host of health-related issues. Fitness is one example. Why do we see couch potatoes pounding the pavement on New Year's Day, only to see them disappear by Valentine's Day? Poor fitness levels, like weight, are the result of poor choices made over time. Going from nothing to a budding marathoner in a day has a high probability of failure. It is far better to start with a walk around the block and build up your activity as your fitness improves. Why? Small lifestyle changes, over time, are easier to implement and have a higher probability of success. I believe in stacking the odds in your favour whenever you can. The simple fact that you have now taken some of your time (your most valuable asset) and allocated it to improving your fitness is a positive lifestyle change. The old saying that "you have to learn to walk before you can run" holds true here too. First you walk. Then you walk fast. Then you can run. The most important thing is that you have adjusted your lifestyle to allocate some of your time to your fitness level—not that you became an Ironman in a month.

Getting personal health on track is critical to long-term happiness. Studies have shown that even people who become physically disabled are able to return to their original levels of happiness quite quickly. It's not disability, but chronic ill health that is the problem. If you have good health, then keep it. If you're overweight, unfit, or a smoker, then fix it.

"Be yourself; everyone else is taken."
—Oscar Wilde

The *philosophical* part of life relates to the value systems that guide our lives. We all have a set of values by which we live. Those values may have been derived from the beliefs of a formal religion. They may have been learned through input from our parents, our teachers, our peers, society, the media, or from our own searches for meaning. We all have a need to pause, reflect, and find meaning in the world around us. Our value systems help us do this.

Each of us has a philosophical foundation and structure that drives how we think about things. What traits do you believe are important for people to have in this life? How do you believe we should all behave? What is the right thing to do—and what is wrong? What traits do you like to see in others? What are the traits you believe others see in you? What traits do you believe "successful" people have? Thinking through these questions, and others like them, will begin to give you a sense of your value system. Gaining an understanding of the values underlying your thought processes is an important starting point in your journey to the life you desire.

One thing is certain. We all have a set of values that drives our own sense of right and wrong, the way we think, and how we make decisions. We may not have thought about our value systems, but we all have them. The philosophical part of life is about the kind of person we'll be.

The Relativities

The balance we choose within each of these five key areas of life will vary in our own searches for prosperity, happiness, contentment, or whatever label we apply to our desired visions for the outcomes of our lives. However, the relative importance of the five areas will be similar for each of us.

An individual's philosophical foundation is essential because everything else will be built on that foundation. The relational and physical areas of our lives are the next two most important areas. Health and the quality of our relationships determine how we feel about our lives. The financial and occupational areas of our lives are of less importance, yet they will get the greatest focus from the average person.

You can be broke and unemployed and still be happy. However, if your health is a slow-moving train wreck and your relationships are a disaster, you have no chance at happiness. In addition, if the relational and physical areas of your life are in trouble, it is very likely that the occupational and financial areas of your life will also suffer. If you think you need more money to be happy, you need to travel more. Some of the happiest people you will ever meet are in some of the poorest countries you will ever travel to. Beyond survival needs, money will never make you happier than you are today. It may give you different choices— but not greater happiness.

"Be the change that you wish to see in the world."
—Mahatma Gandhi

In order for us to be happy, we must take a holistic approach to life. That means that we must have a balance between each of the five key areas of life. Each of us must determine what the right balance is for us, but there must be a degree of balance in each area for us to maintain a sense of well-being and contentment. Any on-going deficiency in one area of life will eventually unbalance the other areas. We cannot neglect one part of our lives without that neglect eventually having a negative impact on some other part.

Within each of these five key areas, we must determine whether the balance is right and whether each of these parts of our lives is heading in the right direction.

CHAPTER 4

Alternation, the First Other "Force"

"The race is not to the swift or the battle to the strong, nor does food come to the wise or wealth to the brilliant or favour to the learned; but time and chance happen to them all."
—Ecclesiastes 9:11

Alternation is defined as successive change from one thing or state to another and back again. This is the first other force capable of impacting the direction of your motion through life. The principle of alternation has been around for thousands of years. In the East, it is known as yin and yang. The Greek Heraclites described it as the unity of opposites. In more recent times, Marx and Engels described this principle as the law of polarity.

You should think of the principle of alternation as the cycles of life. Life is based on a variety of cycles or rhythms. Some of these cycles are regular, for instance day and night. Some cycles are more irregular, for instance the El Niño and La Nina weather patterns. Other examples of the principle of alternation would be winter and summer, hot and cold days, floods and drought, sunshine and rain, feasts and famine.

Our difficulties begin when we falsely believe that somehow we are not subject to these same cycles or rhythms of life. The fact is that we all have good days and bad days. We also have days when our energy is high and days when our energy is low. Sometimes we experience good luck, and sometimes we experience bad luck. Sometimes we feel positive about the future, and sometimes we feel negative about it.

It is important for us to realize that we are not the centre of the universe, but only a very small part of it. Sometimes we get so immersed in the seeming importance of our own lives that we forget that there are more than seven billion people who don't know we even exist. If you or I were hit by a bus tomorrow, there are more than seven billion people who wouldn't know anything about it. The "world" is neither for us nor against us. The "world" is ambivalent towards us, as is "life," "society," or any other global term that we sometimes like to blame things on. The world is neither moral nor immoral. The world is amoral. It's not that the world doesn't care about us—it's just that the "world" has no awareness of us.

Everyone has an allotted share of good news and bad news in life. During our lives, we will all experience frustration, disappointment, heartache, and despair. Everyone will suffer painful life events. The difference is whether we make them our servants or our masters. The issue is not whether we will experience these things, but what we will do when we experience them. We will all face similar situations and circumstances during the course of our lives, but the choices we make at the times we face these problems will have the greatest impact on the direction our lives take in the aftermath. We must keep moving towards our desired destinations since all cycles, good and bad, will pass. Perhaps the best thing to keep in mind is an old Hebrew saying. King Solomon said, "And this too shall pass."

Challenges and obstacles are not reserved for any particular group of people. We have all had situations turned to dust right before our eyes, despite all of our plans and best efforts. Rich or poor, educated or uneducated, employed or unemployed, single or married, fat or thin, happy or unhappy, we all have problems during the course of our lives.

The principle of alternation dictates that we will all have challenges and opportunities in our lives. Like the weather, we will have sunny days and rainy days. Sometimes we get both in the same day. It doesn't matter whether we aim high or low in life, we will still have good days and bad days. That's how life works. No matter what we choose to do in life, we will be challenged. The greater the things we want to achieve in life, the greater the obstacles life will seem to put in our path. People who succeed in life are willing to work to overcome bigger obstacles, than those who don't. The choice then is how big a rainstorm we are willing to endure to get what we want out of life.

Some people will struggle through their challenges and come out the other side bigger and better than when they went in. Others will seem to get stuck in their problems and never come out the other side at all. The reality is that there are no "great" people, only ordinary people who overcome "great" obstacles. "Greatness" is achieved by simply doing what other people believe you cannot do.

When life knocks you down (and it will), when you think you just can't go on (and you will), when it seems that no matter what you do is wrong (and that will happen too), the only thing that will get you up off your knees and back on your feet will be knowing that you have a specific destination to reach—and that you will get there in the end. Without a destination, you have no direction to go, and without a direction to go, the circumstances of life will push you to places you never wanted to be.

"I am not judged by the number of times I fail, but
by the number of times I succeed; and the number

of times I succeed is in direct proportion to the
number of times I can fail and keep on trying."
—Tom Hopkins

The degree of success you have in life will be directly proportional to the number of problems you solve and obstacles you overcome. Your measure of success is not whether you have a problem, but whether it's the same problem you had last year. If you are constantly facing the same problem, it is likely that you haven't found the right solution.

The ability to persist towards your desired destination, in the face of adversity, is a key factor in every success story you will ever read. However, persistence should never be confused with stubbornness. I'm sure you've all heard Einstein's famous definition of insanity: Doing the same thing over and over again, expecting a different result. Stubbornness is continually banging your head on the wall in the vain hope that the wall will eventually give way.

Persistence is when you know that you must find a way through, over, under, or around the wall to reach your desired destination—and continuing to search for the best solution. You must always persist in the pursuit of your desired aim, but be flexible in how you go about pursuing it. If you truly want to do something in life, you'll find a way. If you don't, you'll find an excuse.

"It does not matter how slowly you go
as long as you do not stop."
—Confucius

The key to resolving problems and overcoming obstacles is to accept them as yours, to own them. Once you "own" something, you can do what you want with it. Ownership gives you the freedom to do what's required to resolve any issue. Too many people go through life complaining without being prepared to do something, preferring to blame others or circumstances. Nothing will change by complaining about your relationships, your work, your finances, your health, or anything else. Change will only occur when you accept the problem as your problem and take action to resolve it. The simple fact is that you cannot change another human being. You can only change yourself. You must take responsibility for your life and what you want out of it. No one else will. Personal power comes from personal responsibility.

It's important that we keep perspective. It's not what happens to us in life that's important; how we react to what happens to us is what matters. When we're in darkness, there is daylight elsewhere in the world. When we're at work, others are resting. When it's raining, the sun is shining somewhere. When things aren't going well for us, they are for someone else.

You cannot control life. The reality is that the principle of alternation virtually guarantees that your well-laid "plan" to achieve your desired aim will need to change. It will require you to be flexible and to adapt to changing circumstances. Events that are outside your ability to control are a fact of life. Just as surfers can't control the waves, you can't control life. However, good surfers learn to master the waves that the ocean throws at them, and you must learn to master whatever life throws at you.

It's important to remember that the principle of alternation dictates that there will be cycles in each of our lives. Because of this, we must remain focused on the direction towards our desired destinations. There are no straight lines in nature. Straight lines are a man-made phenomenon. That is why knowing your direction in life is so important. It's not the direction of today or yesterday that matters. It's the trend in the direction of your life that's important. Life will not always go the way we want, or hope it will, every day. It is said that experience is what you get when you don't get what you want. However, by remaining focused on the direction our lives are heading, and making adjustments to that direction as required, our motion will continually trend towards what we're striving to achieve in life.

CHAPTER 5

Volition, the Most Important Other "Force"

"Nothing is more difficult, and therefore more
precious, than to be able to decide"
—Napoleon Bonaparte

Volition is the second other force impacting your life, and it is by far the most important. Volition is the capability of conscious choice, decision, and intention—the act of making a choice. It is the exercise of free will.

Volition gives us the power to maximize the advantages from the good things that happen to us in life while minimizing the damages from the bad things. It is a wild card that gives us the ability to maximize the benefits of the law of motion. It is how we counteract the unexpected events thrown at us by the principle of alternation. To put it bluntly, volition gives us the ability to "grab the advantage and cut the damage." The ability to make choices is the most powerful tool we have for achieving the things we want to achieve in life.

However, the power to choose carries a conundrum with it. A conundrum is a puzzle, a paradoxical dilemma, or an enigma. The *volition conundrum* is that while you have the ability to choose, you don't have a choice not to choose. In other words, at every decision point in your life, a choice is made. It will either be an *active* choice or a *passive* choice. That is the conundrum. If you choose not to choose, you've chosen. Indecision is a decision.

You must work to avoid making passive choices in life. For instance, if you can't decide whether to start that new exercise program, then the result is the same as if you had chosen not to start it. If you can't decide whether or not to put your hand up for that new job, then the result is the same as if you had chosen not to try for it. The same applies to beginning a new personal budget, a new diet, a new friendship, a new hobby, or any other change of direction in your life. Not deciding is the same as deciding not to.

To use a simple example, if you roll a ball across the floor it will be subject to the law of motion. The law of motion will dictate that the ball will roll in a straight line. The ball will also be subject to the principle of alternation. For instance, as it is rolling along the floor, it may bump against an obstacle, and that obstacle (another force) will cause it to change direction. The ball has no volition. Being inanimate, it does not have the ability to choose to change direction or go around the obstacle. Unlike us, it can't choose a different path. If you choose not to choose, you become like the ball. Indecision is a passive choice.

Success or failure in life is the result of a chain of choices, be they active or passive choices. James Rohn said, "You will either live a life of choice or a life of chance." A life driven by indecision, or passive choices, means that your life will be a life of chance, dictated by the principle of alternation. Like the ball above, if you choose not to choose, the direction of your life will be decided by the obstacles you bump into.

Where you are today is the result of every decision you have made in your life up to this point. At birth, there are an infinite number of paths your life could take. As you move through life, the choices you make affect the types and numbers of paths available to you.

It is important here to recognize that your past does not equal your future. Your past is your history. Your past is where you made previous choices. Your past is known. Your future is unknown; it is where you have yet to make choices. While we know what has happened in the past, we can only assume what may happen in the future.

The present is where your past meets your future. It is the only place where we can make choices and take action. The present represents only a moment in time. One moment, it is the future; the next it is the present, and then it is the past. Just as your past is the sum total of your previous choices, your future will be the result of your future choices. In other words, just as you have chosen your past, you will choose your future. True power lies in accepting that you are the cause of your own results to this point.

We all make choices every day—from when we get out of bed, to what we'll eat, to when we'll go to work or school, to how much effort we'll put in while we're there, to when we'll go home, to what exercises we'll do, to how we'll spend our evening, and on and on.

Too often, we fail to think about the choices we make; we tend to make a lot of them out of habit. The issue is whether these "habitual" choices are serving us well as we pursue better lives. We need to look at the habitual or unconscious choices we make daily to determine whether they are taking us in the direction we want to go. Habits are simply well-worn ways of thinking and the way we think is what makes us who we are. In order to "move" from where we are to where we want to be, we need to make sure that our habits are working in our own best interests.

"The life which is not examined is not worth living."
—Plato

To do this, we need to go through a period of self-examination. We need to stop stumbling blindly through our years on earth and ask ourselves if the time we are spending is time well spent. We need to step off the treadmill that our lives have become and take a hard look at each and every choice we make. We need to focus on taking our habitual and unconscious choices and turning them into conscious choices. We need to examine the choices we make every day and decide whether they are supporting us in the long-term quest to achieve our ultimate visions or if they are only giving us a dose of short-term gratification.

Too often, we confuse true happiness with short-term gratification. Having the chocolate cake makes us feel good for the moment, but it simply adds to our feelings of guilt and discontent about our on-going struggle to lose weight. Watching the TV after a hectic day may sound good at the moment, but it's not as good for you as a walk around the block.

Where we are in life is not the result of some great cosmic accident—it is the result of the thousands of choices we have made in life up to this point. If the choices we have made to this point aren't serving us well, we need to make different choices. In order to make different choices, we need to look at the kinds of choices we are "habitually" making and choose better ones.

"Every man is born as many men and dies as a single one."
—Martin Heidegger

Think of a gigantic tree of life with thousands of individual branches leading off of the trunk into many more thousands of individual twigs. At birth, you have all the various branches and twigs to choose from. As you start out in life, you are traveling from ground level up through the trunk. As an infant and in your early years, traveling up the trunk, you really don't have the opportunity to make many choices, so there are no branches to choose from. The branches start coming along during your school years and beyond. Each branch you choose leads you towards other branches to choose from as you move through life. Each branch you choose takes you into a different part of the tree and towards a different set of future branches to choose from. While lots of branches will still make their way to the top of the tree, some will provide a more direct path than others, and others will never get to the top at all. The further you go along your chosen path, the fewer branches you will have left to choose from in the future. Eventually, as you reach the end of your journey through life, you will look back and be able to see the path that your choices took you through the tree of life. Out of all the thousands of different paths you could have taken, you will have chosen only one. That is why the choices we make each day are so very important. Each choice moves us into a different part of the tree, and we must be sure that it's a part of the tree we want to be in.

You must begin thinking of choices as possibility filters. The choices you make in the present will either narrow or expand the opportunities you have in the future. Each choice helps to create the future you desire or to destroy it. There is no middle ground. You are either moving towards what you want or away from it. There are many "futures" available to you. There are probable futures, possible futures and, of course, your preferred future. Which "future" you will end up living in is being decided with each and every choice you make, each day, in each "present" moment.

PART 2

How "Life" Impacts You

Part 2 of this book will show you how the principles discussed in part 1 actually work in the real world. Using the knowledge you have gained from part 1, you will begin to understand why things happen as they do. This is where theory meets practical application.

CHAPTER 6

Our Value Systems

"When I let go of what I am, I become what I might be."
—Lao Tzu

What drives the way we make decisions? What is behind the choices we make in life? The choices we make in life are driven largely by our philosophical beliefs. Philosophical is the fifth key area of life; it is the foundation of who we are and is the major determinant of an individual's direction in life.

The philosophical part of life is the value system that underpins our beliefs and is the major driver of the choices we make. Values are about who you want to be—rather than what you want to achieve. They are the guiding principles that motivate you and provide direction in life. Values create a framework for us to operate in. They give context and meaning to the world around us. The meaning that our values give to "events" in the world creates the feelings or emotional states that we then attach to those "events." Our value systems tell us what the world is like and how we should behave in it.

Unlike goals, values have no endpoint. For example, the values of being kind, creative, and adventurous translate into goals like volunteering, taking an art class, or going on a trip to South America. We must first uncover our values. Once we understand our value systems, we can create visions for our lives that align with those values.

It is important to understand that you will not be able to achieve your vision of your ideal life if it is in conflict with your value system. Your value system will drive the decisions that you make, and those decisions, those choices, are what will move you towards or away from the vision you have of your ideal life. Your value system must be compatible with your desired vision. Too many people go through life with a constant feeling of dissatisfaction or an on-going sense of discontent because they are trying to live a life in conflict with their value system.

Most of us have never really given any thought to our underlying value systems—or how they came into being—even though value systems make us who we are. Our values come to us in many ways and operate on both the conscious and subconscious levels. They are formed differently at different stages in our lives.

During a person's *imprint period*, which is up until about the age of seven, the subconscious mind does not have the capability to filter out any facts or opinions others may have about us or the world we live in. In order to be able to filter out facts or opinions we don't agree with, the subconscious mind must have a benchmark with which to compare these facts or opinions. During that stage, there is no filter on the subconscious mind because people don't have existing value systems to filter the incoming information. During this early period, the initial value system is being formed. During these formative years, we are literally blank slates that others write upon. In other words, the subconscious mind simply accepts what is presented to it. During that period, parents—and to a lesser extent, siblings— have the greatest influence on the formation of an individual's value system.

In the *modelling period*—between the ages of about seven and fourteen—the people affecting the continuing evolution of our value system expands to include teachers, friends, and heroes, in addition to the continuing influence of family. By this stage, a person's value system begins filtering some of the feedback it receives if it does not align with how he or she believes things are or should be. This is called the modelling period, because we do, in fact, begin modelling some of the behaviours and thought patterns that we're continuously exposed to. At this stage in a child's life, parents may say, "Do as I say, not as I do." Children don't yet know that some of the behaviours we may be exhibiting aren't socially acceptable. I think most parents have had this phrase said to them as children—and said it to their own children. The question is whether the behaviour a child is modelling is even appropriate for adults or if it is something we exhibit unconsciously and need to change.

The *socialization period*—from about fourteen to twenty-one—is characterized by a further expansion of those people impacting the continuing evolution of a person's value system. These new contributors come to us mainly through different forms of media. They may include political figures, celebrities, TV personalities, sporting figures, and other media types.

After the age of twenty-one, we have created a fairly well-established value system, whether we are conscious of it or not. Whether this value system is serving us well is a different proposition. This is not to say that a person's value system ceases to evolve after the age of twenty-one, but from this time on, we are the greatest contributor to its makeup. We take control of the on-going evolution of our individual value system. As people grow older, outside influences play an increasingly diminishing role in the evolution of their value systems.

"It is never too late to be what you might have been."
—George Eliot

I hope that you caught the continuing use of the term "evolution" in discussing your value system. At no point in time does it become set in stone—unless you choose to make it so. If your current value system is not taking you where you want to go in life, you can change it. There is nothing stopping you from adopting new values or elevating some values to a more important place in your value system. We'll discuss core and secondary values in a later chapter, but suffice it to say at this point, that you can become "who" you need to become to achieve "what" you want to achieve.

If you want to get an initial snapshot of the shape of your value system, perhaps the best place to start is to answer a question posed by Albert Einstein. He said, "The most fundamental decision you have to make in your life is this . . . do I live in a friendly or a hostile universe?" As a starting point, there is no better question to ask yourself. The answer to this question will give you a sense of the beliefs, attitudes, and meanings that your current value system is providing you.

It's easy to see how the answer to this question can shine a light on your underlying value system. For instance, you can easily see how something as simple as "trusting others" is different if you live in a friendly versus a hostile universe. If you live in a friendly universe, you will find it relatively easy to trust others until they prove themselves not to be trustworthy. However, if you live in a hostile universe, you won't trust anyone until they prove they can be trusted.

This elemental distinction—of a hostile versus a friendly world—carries through to every part of your life. How different is the perception of the world between those of us who believe we live in a friendly universe and those who believe they live in a hostile one?

The starting point for anyone serious about making changes in life is to look at the values underpinning their beliefs and attitudes. Your value system is the only place in which you can begin making permanent changes in your life, and we will examine it in part 3 of this book.

What all of this means is that from a relatively young age, we have the control and the ability to change our value systems—or any part of them—if they are not serving us well. This is critically important because who we are, where we are, what we believe, and how we think are driven by our individual value systems.

CHAPTER 7

TAR

"It is a painful thing to look at your own troubles and to know
that it is you yourself, and no one else, who has made it"
—Sophocles (born 495 BC)

TAR stands for *thought, action, result.* TAR is life's feedback loop.
You can almost think of this in terms of a "Circle of Results."
As discussed in the previous chapter, our value systems give
meaning to life's events. This meaning creates an emotional
state or feeling. These feelings, in turn, lead to us thinking about
these events in a certain way. Those thoughts drive our decisions,
actions, and behaviours. Those actions will then produce
specific results in the real world. Those results will impact how
we feel, which will then lead to further thoughts—and the circle
continues.

Thought

Perception is everything. How we perceive the world around us
colours the meanings we attach to events. In essence, everything
is meaningless until we attach a meaning to it. No specific event
has any inherent meaning.

As an example, let's take the story of the "Farmer and the Bride." This simple story illustrates how two different people will have two very different reactions to the same event. A young bride has spent the last six months anxiously preparing for her wedding day. She's organized everything to perfection. The wedding will be held at a local park that sits on top of a hill just outside town. It's a beautiful place that overlooks the entire valley. In fact, from this vantage point, you can see the town and all the surrounding farmland.

The young bride's wedding day is a celebration that most of the people in the town have been looking forward to. The valley has been struggling through a drought for five years. At this point in time, everyone could use a good celebration. Finally, the big day arrives. Everything is going exactly as planned. However, by mid-afternoon, the sky has darkened, and then one of the biggest thunderstorms that anyone can remember rolls through the valley. Everyone and everything gets soaked. The bride is in tears. Her day is ruined. Just down the hill, the farmer rushes outside and stands with his face turned up towards the rain. He's also in tears, but his are tears of joy because now his crop will be saved—and so will his family farm. One freak rainstorm, two people in tears; one tears of joy, the other, tears of despair. It's the same event, but there are two very different perceptions of it. Perceptions are everything.

As humans, we have an instinctual need to attach meanings to things. This need is a leftover part of humanity's "survival instinct." At a time in the dim, dark past, knowing what certain things meant could be critical for survival. While this survival instinct is less important to us today, the need to attach meanings to things remains. The meaning we attach to things helps us understand the world. It determines how we make sense of what happens around us.

An event has meaning once we attach one to it. The meanings we attach to events determine how we feel about those events; our value systems and beliefs determine the meanings we attach to the events. It follows then that in order to change our world, we must change how we view the world. And the only way we can do that is to change our value systems. By changing our value systems, we change the way we believe the world operates. By changing our beliefs, we can change the meanings we attach to things.

If I think back to my early days at university, I have to laugh. I remember many late-night drinking sessions being taken up with discussions about the meaning of life. It took me a great many years to realize that life itself has no meaning. The only meaning that life has is the meaning that you give to it—and that meaning comes from what you choose to do with it. You change the direction of your journey through life by seeing the world through new eyes—not by seeking a new world

You don't need a new job, a new partner, a new house, or different things to change your direction in life. You need a new you. By changing your value system, you become a different person—and the world around you changes too. When you change, your world changes. Reality is subjective. "Your" world is unique to you. It is the result of how you think, and how you think is driven by your values.

We can readily see reflections of our current value systems in the quality of our self-talk. There is a running commentary in each of our heads from the moment we wake up until we fall asleep at night. Some choose to call this the "monkey mind" because it chatters all day long. Your mind never rests. If your daily mental commentary is peppered with phrases like, "How could I be that stupid?" "I'm too old to try that," "Everyone's against me," "You just can't trust anyone," "I'll never be able to do that," "That's too hard," "I'm just too tired," etc., how can you possibly hope to do the things you will need to do to make positive changes in your life?

If you really want to get a picture of your current value system and whether it is supporting you in your journey to a better life, listen to your self-talk for a day. Really listen to what thoughts are running through your mind as you go through the day. Think about the sorts of values and beliefs that underlie that kind of thinking.

What we think—self-talk—is a by-product of the value system we have developed over the course of our lives. If, like me, you were brought up in a home where you were consistently reminded of your faults, mistakes, and short-comings (just to make sure that you didn't get too full of yourself), then maintaining a positive self-image and uplifting self-talk can be a lifelong struggle. To be fair, parents will often provide critical feedback, believing that this will motivate you to do better the next time, but many don't sprinkle that criticism with a healthy dose of praise for your successes and abilities. In life, we need both constructive criticism and praise if we hope to continue to develop and improve ourselves.

"All that we are arises with our thoughts. With
our thoughts, we make the world"
—Gautama Buddha

The most important thing for each of us to remember is that the only opinion that really matters is the one you have about yourself. You are the only one responsible for your life. No one else will be held accountable for your actions. No one else will reap the results that flow from your actions. Therefore, no one else's opinion about you is more important than your own.

If your self-talk is consistently negative, how can you expect to forge ahead into uncharted waters, try something new, or break out of your comfort zone? We must learn to recognize that the most important conversations we have each day are the ones we have with ourselves through our thoughts.

Each of us must learn to be supportive of our own efforts, to praise ourselves (when praise is due), and to see how we could have improved our results if they weren't what we wanted. We all know that we enjoy being around someone who praises us, recognizes our successes, is happy to see us, or genuinely makes us feel good about ourselves. That person should be you. We shouldn't have to look outside ourselves to find the person who builds us up and makes us feel that we can achieve the things we set out to achieve in life. We need to become our own best cheerleaders.

Positive self-talk will, over time, help us develop self-belief. Self-belief is not something we come into this world with. It's something that we develop—or fail to develop—as we travel through life. Developing self-belief is not easy in this day and age, but it is extremely important in the quest to improve how we think and the quality of our lives.

Action

Our thoughts drive the decisions we make. The things in life we choose to do—or choose not to do—follow from how we think about those things. Once we have taken control of the way we view the world and how we think about it, we can begin to do things differently. Because we now think differently, we can begin to act differently. Our actions are the outward manifestations of how we think.

The law of attraction has its origins in the Hindu concept of "like attracts like." It has been proposed by some New Age thinkers that the law of attraction means that all we have to do is think about what we desire and it will come to us. Some would like you to believe that if you were to simply focus your thoughts on receiving a bag of money that somehow that bag of money will magically appear before you. This is clearly untrue.

No matter how much you might focus your mind on receiving a bag of money, it's not going to fall out of the sky and hit you on the head. There are plenty of bags of money in the world, but you must go—through your actions—to where the bags of money are. You must become the sort of person who does the sort of things that would attract a bag of money. The Bible says, "Seek and ye shall find." It doesn't say think about it and it will come. We've all played hide-and-seek as children. The person doing the seeking had to go out and find the person doing the hiding. You didn't wait for them to come to you; you took action to find them.

The truth is that you must become like the thing you desire—not the other way around. All things are already here. If the thing you desire isn't in your life now, that is because you are not like it. You must become the person that is like it. Through your thoughts and actions, you must become the sort of person who would naturally have whatever it is that you desire.

The law of attraction can best be illustrated like this. If I were to place a ball in the middle of the room, and I sat in the corner and visualized the ball in my hand, no matter how much thought and focus I brought to bear, the ball would not appear in my hand. If I want the ball in my hand, I must get up, go to where the ball is, and pick it up. It is up to me to take the action required to get the ball. It can't be made any clearer than that. If I am attracted to something that is not currently in my world, I must go to where that thing is. In other words, I must turn my world into the kind of world where the thing I want exists.

When the Maharishi Mahesh Yogi was raising funds for a new spiritual centre, he was asked where he thought he'd get the money from. He answered, "We'll get it from wherever it is now." The things that we want in this world, whatever they may be, are already here. These things—inanimate objects like money, houses, and cars—or less concrete things like better health, better relationships, or a happier life already exist in the world. All the things we desire in life are already here. We must become the sort of person whose world contains those things.

"Things" lack volition. Therefore, they can't choose a new direction. They can't choose to move towards you. So, the problem isn't that they don't exist. The problem is that they don't exist in "your" world. You must move towards them by changing the way you think and the things you do. By changing the way that you think, it is not that the things you want will come to you, but that you will move towards them.

We have volition. We have the ability to choose new directions, and our actions move us in those directions. The secret is not that the things will come to us, but that we will go to the things. In order to get the things you want in life, you must become the person that those things belong to. Thought without action is just a fantasy. You cannot plough a field by turning it over in your mind. To move in the direction you want your life to go, thought and action must be used together.

> "Winners take imperfect action, while
> losers are still perfecting the plan."
> —Anthony Robbins

Successful people take action. They don't procrastinate. Procrastination takes many forms: lack of a firm direction, over-analysis, lacking the discipline to get started, or a perceived lack of ability or resources. The most common types of fear are the fear of commitment, the fear of the unknown, and the fear of failure.

Fear of commitment frightens a lot of people. Any kind of change takes commitment, and commitment to make a change forces us to take a hard look at ourselves. It forces us to ask uncomfortable questions, such as "What is it that I really want?" and "What am I willing to do to make that change a reality?" and "Is that going to be enough to make it happen?" Comments such as "I'll try" or "I'll see how it goes" are normally code words for a fear of commitment and virtually doom the contemplated change to failure.

Fear of the unknown is probably the most common fear. Unfortunately, this is programmed into the subconscious. Any time we seek to venture out of the known (a person's comfort zone), we face an underlying sense of misgiving about the potential outcomes. This is absolutely normal and must be overridden by conscious discipline if you are to move ahead. Back in cave-dweller days, this fear of the unknown was often a lifesaver and was not to be ignored. Unfortunately, it is still hanging around today—even when there aren't any sabre-toothed tigers waiting to jump out of the bushes at us.

Whenever you seek to move out of your comfort zone and make a change, you won't be sure what the new future will look like. This lack of surety will likely make you feel uncomfortable. You must replace this discomfort with an inspiring picture, in your mind, of what the outcome of this change will mean to you and how important it is for you to begin living in this new future. All positive changes result in personal growth.

Fear of failure is also a very common fear. Change is a process, and it never moves in a straight line. Any time you attempt to make changes, you will experience setbacks. It is irrational to believe that everything will just fall into place once you decide to make a change. It won't. You will have lots of little failures on your way to ultimate success.

Don't expect to be good at something the first time you try it. The only way to experience ultimate failure is to give up. There will be lots of obstacles between where you are now and where you want to ultimately be. Accept these obstacles as a necessary part of your journey to success.

"One can choose to go back towards safety or forward towards growth. Growth must be chosen again and again. Fear must be overcome again and again."
—Abraham Maslow

The fact is that you will never be short of a reason or excuse not to move forward if that is what you want. But is it? In order to figure out how to steer a bicycle, you must first begin pedalling. You can't steer a stationary bike. In order to move towards whatever your objective is, you must first begin moving. Will your initial movement be perfect? Absolutely not. No one jumps on a bicycle and rides perfectly right from the start, but as you continue moving forward, you get better at making sure you're going in the direction you want to go.

We have all probably witnessed a baby learning to walk. They get up, they fall down, they get back up, they fall back down, and it goes on and on until eventually they learn how to walk. They don't "try." They don't just "give it a shot." They don't "see how it goes." They just keep doing it until they get it right. They didn't jump up and do it perfectly right from the start. We were all there once ourselves; why is it that as we grow up, we get this idea that we need everything to be perfect before we even try it. If we aren't experts on day one, that doesn't mean we should just give up.

Most successful people are successful because they were willing to get it wrong while they learned how to get it right. They were willing to make more mistakes than the other guy as they learned how to do it better. Winners accept failure, and failures don't. Successful people realize that if you wait until all the traffic lights are green, you will never begin the journey. If the first traffic light is green, you can get started. The rest of the lights will get sorted out in due course.

Greg Norman tells the story of the group of boys he started playing golf with. When they were young, he wasn't even one of the best in the group. However, he out-practiced, outlasted and eventually outplayed his contemporaries. Greg Norman continued working on his skills until he became one of the best in the world. It wasn't his "natural" skill that made him better than they were, because the other boys were "naturally" better when they all started out playing together. It was simply that he had the tenacity, persistence, and discipline to keep working at it when the others stopped.

If there is something you know you need to do and are procrastinating on getting started, then that is the time that self-discipline comes into its own. It is the one thing that will get you to take that first step. If there is one single trait that successful people have that unsuccessful people don't, it's self-discipline. The ability to do the things you really don't want to do is the key to your future success. Whether it's exercising even though you're tired and it's cold, not eating that thing you'd really like to eat, or making that phone call you'd really rather not make, self-discipline is what will get you over the line.

"Discipline is the bridge between goals and accomplishment."
—James Rohn

The beauty of self-discipline is that anyone can develop it. Just like learning to walk or ride a bike, it takes patience, persistence, and small steps in the beginning. While your goal might be to run a marathon, first just walk around the block. While your goal might be to lose twenty kilograms, first just give up dessert two days a week. First conquer the small things—and then move on to the next slightly bigger thing. If you don't have it, self-discipline, like any other muscle, must be developed one small step at a time.

Start developing your self-discipline "muscle" today with something small and simple. By doing this, you will create a track record of success that will take you to whatever heights you choose to go to in the years ahead.

Results

Our results are the feedback we receive, from life, for the actions we have taken. How we think drives what we do. What we do produces results in the real world. Through our results, we are able to determine whether our lives are moving in the direction we want them to.

It is simple really. If you want to lose weight and yet your weight continues to increase, then, logically, you are doing the wrong things. In order to lose weight, you must start doing something differently. If you want to save money and yet you continue to go deeper into debt, then, logically, you are doing something wrong and must change your behaviour. If you want to increase your fitness but seem to get more and more out of shape, then you must change what you are doing. Your results are direct, honest, objective feedback from life as to whether your actions and your desires are aligned. If your results are not what you're after, then your current actions must change.

There is really no such thing as success or failure—there are only results. Success and failure are just the labels we use to describe our perception of the results we achieved from a particular action. Life is simple. We think, we act, and we get results. Results are merely the feedback life gives us. We choose to label good results as successes and bad results as failures. Life just looks at them all as results. We should too.

Results are like signposts showing us where we're going. Results show us whether our thoughts and our actions are aligned with the directions we want our lives to go. The beauty is that life doesn't have it in for us. Life isn't trying to keep us from getting where we want to go. Life doesn't even know what direction you want to go. Frankly, life doesn't know the difference between success and failure. Life just *is*.

If you want to change the way you think about life and failure, try this. Life is actually trying to help us by letting us know if we're heading in the right direction. If the results we are getting are not taking us where we want to go, we simply need to change the way we think. Our thoughts, the way we think about things, determine the actions we take. If these actions result in the wrong results, we need to start back at the beginning and change the thoughts that led to those actions by changing the values and beliefs that drove those thoughts.

You can't keep doing the same thing and hope to get a different result. If your results are not the results you want, your actions have to change. In order for your actions to change, you have to change the way you think. In order to change the way you think, you must change the way you see the world—and the ability to do that is found in changing your value system.

In order to take control of your life, you must take control of how you think. Your results don't lie. They are an objective measure of the direction your life is taking. Some people choose not to look at their results; instead, they come up with reasons for their results. Reasons are just excuses. Reasons are justifications that allow us to think that somehow the results are wrong. The results aren't wrong. In fact, results are neither right nor wrong. The results are simply the results.

Victims prefer to look for reasons for their results. By making excuses for your results, you are simply giving up control of your life. By making excuses, you are saying that you have no control over your life. While the principle of alternation dictates that, at times, things may happen that are out of your control, it is never an on-going feature of your journey through life. If your results are consistently different than the results you're trying to achieve, it is not as a result of the principle of alternation. It is as a result of your thinking.

> "I have not failed. I've just found ten
> thousand ways that won't work."
> —Thomas Edison

We've all had "successes" and "failures" in life. One of the first things we must do is stop labelling the results that we don't want as "failures." They are simply another example of what doesn't work. We need to learn from the poor results we achieved and change the thinking that led to those results. In other words, learn what you can from your unsatisfactory results and then move on. Don't try to justify the poor results or pretend they didn't happen because you will just repeat them. In fact, you'll keep repeating them until you learn to change the way you're thinking.

The flip side of this is to celebrate your "successes." These are the results you want to reinforce. These are the results you want to repeat. These are the times that your thoughts were in alignment with the direction you want your life to go. Put simply, learn from poor results so you don't repeat them—and celebrate good results so that you will.

PART 3

How To Benefit from the Way Life Works

Part 3 of this book will show you a few simple things you can do to greatly improve the direction of your life. Using the knowledge you have gained from parts 1 and 2, you will now understand why the techniques discussed in part 3 are so simple—yet so powerful.

While there is always more that can be done, if you only do the exercises outlined here, you will see a marked improvement in the movement of your life towards your desired future.

CHAPTER 8

Changing Direction

"Both success and failure are the result of hundreds of
decisions made over a prolonged period of time."
—James Rohn

The key to successfully changing the direction of your life is to answer three questions. Who am I? Where do I want to go? How am I going to get there? Chapter 9 is dedicated to answering the first question. Chapter 10 answers the second question, and chapters 12 and 13 resolve the third question. This chapter is dedicated to giving you an understanding of what is involved in the process of changing direction.

Given that we are all moving in a certain direction in each of the five key areas of our lives, what is involved in changing that direction if it's not taking us where we want to go?

We can't change the world, but we can change ourselves. By changing ourselves, we change the world we live in; everyone is responsible for working on changing themselves. Your job is *you*. If you're not right, then your relationships, your finances, your health, and your work won't be right either. We can change direction in any one, or even all, of the areas of our lives—and we can do it now. It is simply a matter of creating motion in a new direction.

Changing direction takes effort and education. We must be willing to work and willing to learn. These two things are a prerequisite for achieving success at anything in life.

"One thing only I know, and that is that I know nothing."
—Socrates

In order to move in a new direction, a person must be willing to learn. When Warren Buffett was asked what the average person could do to become rich, he answered, "Invest in your education."

Are you willing to admit that you don't know everything and then go out and find out what it is that you don't know? Are you willing to ask questions of those who are doing it better than you are? Are you willing to watch and copy those people succeeding at whatever it is you are trying to achieve? Are you willing to read and study? Are you willing to accept coaching? In short, are you willing to do whatever it takes to learn what you need to learn to be successful and to continue the process of learning throughout your life?

We must be willing to do whatever it takes to put this new knowledge to work. Are you willing to do the hard work necessary to succeed? Are you willing to try something new—even when you don't feel like trying? Are you willing to do what you know you should do—even when you don't want to do it? Are you willing to push through the discomfort of change? Are you willing to put in the necessary time and effort to grow and develop? Are you willing to do more than others expect of you and for longer? Are you willing to keep practicing when all the others have gone home?

Gaining the necessary education and putting in the necessary effort require action on your part. I have no doubt that some people will learn faster than you will. A person with a higher IQ isn't necessarily smarter than you are—they're just able to learn things faster. This just means that you'll have to put in more effort to learn what you need to learn than they will.

Some people may have natural talents that will make it easier for them to accomplish whatever it is that you are trying to accomplish. This doesn't mean you can't accomplish it—it just means that it may take you longer and require more effort on your part.

"Anyone who stops learning is old, whether at twenty or eighty. Anyone who keeps learning stays young."
—Henry Ford

An unfortunate fact is that most people stopped their education when they stopped going to school. At that point, many people think they know everything they need to know to succeed in life. Unfortunately, the more you think you know, the less you learn. In school, they don't teach you how life works. Continuing your education throughout your life is the only way to change your world for the better—and education isn't an accident. You aren't going to "accidentally" learn how to get what you want out of life. You must seek out the information you need, and you must work diligently to implement it.

Champions are not made during the contest; they are made in training. You don't become a champion by getting lucky. Both good and bad luck will play a part in any great achievement. However, in order to become a champion, you must be prepared to take advantage of any good luck that comes your way; to be prepared, you must have put in the required effort beforehand.

Perhaps one of the best examples of this is the story of Steven Bradbury, the Olympic speed skater. At the 2002 Winter

Olympics, Bradbury won the 1000m short track final, when all of his opponents crashed out in a last corner pile-up. Yes, good luck played a pivotal role in that final race for the gold medal. However, it was the thousands of hours of hard work, over many years, that put Steven Bradbury in that final race, enabling him to compete with a handful of the world's best speed skaters. Had he not learned what he needed to learn, worked hard, and put the effort into his training that becoming a champion required, he never would have been in that final medals race to take advantage of the good luck that came his way—and he never would have won the gold medal.

How do we prepare for success? First, we must know exactly what success looks like for us and what we want to achieve. Then, we must seek out the information that we will need to achieve it. Yes, we all learn from our experiences. However, it is far better, faster, and less painful to learn from the experiences of others. We can do this by listening to the experiences of those who have achieved what we want to achieve or by reading the books written by those who have achieved what we want to achieve. Don't take advice from those who haven't done it. The best education you will ever get will come from those who have already done what you want to do.

While the Internet has increased the accessibility and the proliferation of information, knowledge is still at a premium. Knowledge is useful information that allows you to take action to move in the direction of what you want to achieve in life. Each of us must become an expert at what we want in life, what we need to learn to get it, and how to use that new knowledge to move forward.

CHANGING DIRECTION

"He who labours diligently need never despair; for all things are accomplished by diligence and labour."
—Menander (300 BC)

There is one quality that is critical to putting in the effort necessary to learn what we need to learn and do what we need to do, to achieve what we want in life. That quality is self-discipline. Self-discipline is the foundation upon which everything you create in life is built. There is no substitute for self-discipline. I have said all along that success is simple, but it is not easy.

Self-discipline is what's required to do the simple things, each and every day. If you genuinely want to change the direction of any part of your life, you will need to be disciplined. You will need to be able to do the things that need to be done even when you don't feel like doing them. You will need to be able to say no to that impulse purchase. You will need to be able to find a way to do your exercise even if it's raining. You will need to be able to say no to that second helping of your favourite food. You will need to be able to accept that there will be ups and downs in any relationship—and that you can move forward from both. In short, you must take control of your life and how you look at it.

People make changes in the direction of their lives for one of two reasons; they either become frightened or enlightened. Unfortunately, most people will change only as a result of being frightened—the smoker who quit smoking after he was diagnosed with lung cancer, the overweight person who goes on a diet after he's been told he has diabetes, the person who goes bankrupt before they finally give up on their credit cards, and the person who didn't change his behaviour until after his relationships were permanently damaged. The list goes on and on. It's a sad fact that fear and loss are the motivators that drive the majority of people to make the necessary changes in their life.

It is far better to make enlightened change. This is changing because you've chosen to take your life in a new direction, learned what you needed to learn to do it, and then took action to make it a reality. Enlightened change is positive change, and positive change is far better for you—and everyone around you—than change driven by fear or loss.

In order to make enlightened change, you must be in control of your life. You must be the one who accepts responsibility for what happens in your life. You must be the one who accepts that the results you've achieved so far are a result of the things you have done—and that the things you have done are a result of the way you think. To change your results, you must first change the way you think.

The time to begin is now. There is no perfect time to begin because perfection is an illusion. It simply doesn't exist. Everything in life can be improved upon. Therefore, nothing is perfect. Perfectionists are often great procrastinators. Perfectionist-procrastinators are masters at the collection of information. They can never have enough information and believe that—with just one more bit of data—they will have just what they need to do the perfect job. By delaying making decisions and taking action, they often find themselves in a situation where they end up never having enough time. The fact is that you have all the time you will ever have—right now.

Life, in this day and age, is busy. We all seem to have an ever-expanding list of things to do. We have e-mails coming at an ever-increasing pace, a phone that never seems to stop ringing, and people expecting more and more from us. However, working hard or staying back to finish the project on time isn't a good thing if we created the delay in the first place. When most people refer to themselves as being "under the gun," they want to believe—or they do believe—that the pressure is not of their own making. However, if you look at the situation honestly, the delay often resulted from not taking decisive action when you should have. Instead of being proactive early, you procrastinated until the eventual due date became a critical deadline.

One of the best ways to break the shackles of procrastination is to begin taking small steps towards your goals immediately. You can't steer a bicycle that's not moving. You must start pedalling—and then you can begin steering it in the direction you want to go and begin pedalling faster. People usually procrastinate because of the fear of making a mistake; ironically, that fear only grows as the pressure mounts. Make no mistake. Procrastination leads to nothing but pain.

Experience has shown that when you go after a big goal all at once, you will invariably fall short. If you try to swallow an apple whole, you'll choke. You have to eat it one bite at a time. This same principle applies to achieving the ultimate vision for your life.

Achieving the ultimate vision you have for your life means taking every milestone and making it a small step on the road to your ultimate destination. Every small task or requirement becomes a milestone in itself—and leads you towards achieving your ultimate vision. Using this method, each milestone becomes much more manageable. When mistakes are made, they're usually small ones that are easy to correct. With the achievement of each of these small milestones, you receive positive reinforcement, which motivates you to move onto the next milestone.

If you want to run a 10K, first start by walking around the block. If you want to save $10,000, start by throwing your spare change in a jar every night. As basic as this seems, most frustration and failure is caused by trying to "bite off more than we can chew" or trying to reverse a decade of poor decisions in a month. Give yourself at least half as much time as it took to get where you are to get back to where you want to be. You must pursue your goals, but you need to take it one small step at a time.

CHAPTER 9

Your Values List

"As you climb the ladder of success, make sure
it's leaning against the right building."
—Stephen Covey

The first step in creating your vision of the new direction for your life is the answer to the question *"Who am I?"* and to determine what are the guiding principles of your life. As discussed earlier, we all have a value system within which we operate. A value system is the foundation upon which we build our lives. It encompasses our attitudes, our beliefs, our innate perceptions, and our unconscious or habitual ways of thinking. Our values are what make us who we are. They drive the way we think, which, in turn, drives the things we do and the choices we make. Therefore, determining our values (what we value) is the critical first step in creating a vision for a life that aligns with our value systems.

There is absolutely no use in creating a vision for your life that does not align with your value system. There is nothing more important in life than being true to oneself. In order for us to succeed at whatever we put our minds to, our visions must align with our values. Our values, quite simply, are what we hold to be true, good, and lasting. They are what we hold to be significant in life. They are what we believe to be the way life should be lived. They are not only what we believe—they are *why* we believe it.

Your values will determine the types of people you draw into your life and how you relate to them. Your values will drive you towards certain things in life and away from others. In short, the life you have led up until now is what has flowed from the value system you hold today.

The stronger your values are, the greater their impact will be on your life. Spend the time to give the following values exercise your full attention. There is no shortcut to deciding what values are the cornerstones of your life. You will never be able to do the things you need to do to make your vision a reality if those actions don't align with your values. To achieve your ultimate vision, you must decide which values are an important part of your life now—and which ones need to *become* an important part of your life. Determining your core values, and the secondary values that support them, is the first thing we must do.

Value systems are based around a nucleus of four to six core values, which are supported by a host of secondary values. Our core values are fundamental to who we are. Think of your value system as the foundation upon which you build your life; core values are the cornerstones of that foundation. While secondary values change and develop over time, core values tend to stay with us for large parts of our lives. It is important to determine what these core values are in order to create a vision that is in alignment with them.

> "Whatever you are, be a good one."
> —Abraham Lincoln

From the values list at the end of this chapter, you will find your four to six core values—the ones that are most important to you.

The list is extensive, but it is not exhaustive. You may have a very specific value in your mind that is not on the list. Feel free to add it. From this list of values, you must eventually narrow it down to four to six core values. For many, this will be a very difficult exercise. I cannot stress enough the importance of spending the time required to do this exercise correctly. Don't take any shortcuts. It is critical to spend the time to do it right.

I suggest you use the following process:

Step 1. Go through the entire list once and write down, on a separate sheet of paper, every value that resonates with you, that you feel a connection with, and that you feel are important values to have. This first pass through the list will capture both your core and your secondary values. You will likely find that this first list will also contain values that you believe to have very similar meanings. You should eliminate those with similar meanings by keeping the one that you believe most closely defines what you truly value and putting a line through the others. At this point, you will likely be left with twenty to thirty distinct values on your list.

Step 2. Now the real work begins. You must now go through the list of those twenty to thirty values and begin selecting some that you believe are more important than others. Place a dot, in pencil, next to the possible candidates for your list of core values. These are the values that you feel are more important than some of the others around them.

Step 3. Go through your list again focusing only on the values with dots next to them and decide which are more important than some of the others with dots. Erase the dots on those values that aren't quite as important as some of the other values on your list with dots. You may have to repeat this step and go through your list several times. Through this process of elimination, your core values will begin to emerge. This review process is best done over several days to allow you time to "sleep on it" and confirm your thinking. Don't stop the elimination process until you have removed the dots from all of the values except your final four to six. Put a circle around these final core values; these values are the foundation of who you are.

Whatever you do, don't cut this process short. Everything else we do must flow naturally from our core values. If you are genuine in your desire to be true to yourself and to live the life that you want to live, then give this process the time it deserves.

The following pages have a substantial list of possible values for you to use in completing this exercise. Once you are finished, you will have a list of your core values and the secondary values that support them. At that point, you will know what is important to you as an individual—and you can begin the process of creating a vision for your life that will align with your values. You will know "who" you are. You must then begin deciding where you want to go.

The Values List Process:

1. On a separate sheet of paper, write down twenty to thirty values from the list below that you feel are important to you. These are both your core and secondary values.
2. From your list, place a dot (in pencil) next to those values that you feel are most important.
3. Begin erasing the dots from the values that you feel are less important than some of the others with dots. Continue

doing this until you are left with just four to six core values. Circle those core values.

List of Possible Values

Abundance	Acceptance	Accuracy	Achievement
Adaptability	Adventure	Affluence	Agility
Ambition	Appreciation	Assertiveness	Assurance
Astuteness	Attentiveness	Audacity	Authenticity
Awareness	Balance	Beauty	Benevolence
Boldness	Bravery	Calmness	Camaraderie
Candour	Capability	Carefulness	Caring
Certainty	Challenge	Charm	Cheerfulness
Clarity	Cleanliness	Commitment	Compassion
Composure	Confidence	Congruency	Consciousness
Consistency	Contentment	Contribution	Control
Conviction	Cooperation	Courage	Creativity
Credibility	Curiosity	Decisiveness	Dependability
Desire	Determination	Diligence	Direction
Discipline	Drive	Economy	Education
Effectiveness	Efficiency	Empathy	Encouragement
Energy	Enjoyment	Enthusiasm	Excitement
Expertise	Fairness	Faith	Financial Freedom
Fidelity	Firmness	Fitness	Flexibility
Focus	Forthrightness	Fortitude	Frankness
Friendliness	Frugality	Fulfilment	Fun
Generosity	Genius	Giving	Gratitude
Growth	Happiness	Health	Helpfulness
Honesty	Hopefulness	Humility	Humour
Imagination	Independence	Indomitable	Ingenuity
Innovative	Inquisitiveness	Insightfulness	Inspirational

Integrity	Intensity	Intimacy	Intuition
Inventiveness	Joy	Judgment	Kindness
Knowledge	Leadership	Leverage	Liveliness
Logic	Longevity	Loyalty	Maturity
Mindfulness	Modesty	Motivation	Neatness
Nurture	Openness	Optimism	Passion
Patience	Peace	Persistence	Persuasiveness
Philanthropy	Playfulness	Poise	Potency
Power	Practicality	Pragmatism	Precision
Preparedness	Presence	Proactivity	Professionalism
Progress	Prosperity	Punctuality	Reasonableness
Realism	Recognition	Relaxed	Reliability
Resilience	Resolve	Respect	Resourcefulness
Restraint	Risk	Sacrifice	Satisfaction
Security	Selective	Self-Belief	Self-Awareness
Self-Esteem	Self-Honesty	Self-Control	Sensitivity
Serenity	Simplicity	Sincerity	Skilfulness
Spirituality	Spontaneity	Stability	Strength
Supportive	Thankfulness	Thoroughness	Transformational
Trust	Trustworthy	Truth	Truthfulness
Understanding	Vision	Vitality	Warmth
Winning	Wisdom	Wonder	Youthfulness

CHAPTER 10

Your Vision

"If one does not know to which port one
is sailing, no wind is favourable."
—Lucius Seneca (5 BC-AD 65)

Life is a smorgasbord. There is more to choose from than you could possibly desire. The choices are endless. The richest person in the world can't buy everything there is to buy. The most talented person in the world can't be the best at everything. No one has enough time to do everything that there is to do. You can't have it all, but you can have a lot more than you have now. That is where the second question mentioned in chapter 8 comes into play. *Where do I want to go?*

It is critical to decide what you want to have, be, and do in your life. You must create the ultimate vision for your life. To do this, you must have absolute clarity in what you seek from life. You must have clarity in each of the five key areas of your life. The important questions in these five key areas are:

1. Who are the most important people that I want to be a part of my life, and how do I get/keep those relationships positive and beneficial?

2. Am I doing something worthwhile with my life? Am I adding value to the world around me?
3. How much money do I really need to live the lifestyle I desire?
4. What do I need to do to get/keep my health on the right track?
5. Am I living my life according to the values and beliefs that I feel are important to my peace of mind?

Thoughtful answers to the questions above will begin to give you the clarity you need about where you should be focusing your time and energy to create the life you truly desire—the life that will lead you to a deep sense of fulfilment and true personal prosperity.

"When you're finished changing, you're finished."
—Benjamin Franklin

However, before anyone can begin the process of changing direction, they must determine their ultimate destinations. This is the vision we have for our lives. Until we know where we are going, there is no way we can map out the best route to get there. Therefore, your ultimate vision of your life is the next critical step in moving from where you are to where you want to be. Your vision is about the place you want your journey through life to take you.

Creating and committing to an ultimate vision for your life is vital. Without it, there is no way you will achieve the things you desire in this life. I have used the analogy of life as a journey throughout this book, and it really is just that. If you look at your life as a journey from where you are now to your ultimate destination, which is the vision you have for your life, then it becomes much easier to understand the importance of that vision.

Let's say that you're planning a road trip. The first thing you need to do is decide where you want to go. That is the question for this chapter. You cannot plan a trip from point A to point B until you know where point B is. Unless your desire is to turn your life into one big "mystery trip" where you just show up, have no idea where you're going, and hope for the best, then you need to plan your journey. It's an unfortunate fact that most people will spend more time planning their annual holiday than they'll spend planning their life—the most important journey they'll ever make.

Until you decide what your ultimate destination is, you can't plan your trip. You don't know which direction is the right one to take. You don't know how long the trip is likely to take, what roads you'll need to follow, what clothes to pack, etc. In short, you can't begin your journey until you know your destination.

The vision for your life is really no different. Point A is where you are today. It is the starting point in each of the five key areas of your life. Point B is the ultimate vision you have for your life. It is where you want to be in each of those five key areas. The route you take on your road trip is similar to the direction you want to go in your life. Each of the signposts and junctions you pass along the way are milestones that tell you that you are still progressing in the right direction.

Of course, as in any journey, you'll meet obstacles. On your road trip from point A to point B, you may run into traffic jams, road work, detours, or road closures that slow you down or force you to change direction. The principle of alternation dictates that this may happen. When this happens on your road trip, you have to get out your map and plot a new route.

On your life's journey, you'll also run into obstacles as you begin moving from where you are today towards the ultimate vision you have for your life. I know it's difficult to believe, but obstacles are actually positive signs in your life's journey. Obstacles only appear once you have a vision for your life and begin moving towards it. If you're just wandering aimlessly through life, there are no obstacles because you're not going in any specific direction.

If you approach your life as if any direction will do, the principle of alternation will take control—and you'll be blown around a bit like a sailboat without a rudder. You know where you are, but you have no idea where you'll end up. To follow that path is to live your life like running water. Water always follows the path of least resistance and ends up going downhill to the lowest spot. If you're reading this book, I know that's not the life you want to live.

"Death is not the greatest loss in life. The greatest loss is what dies inside while still alive. Never surrender."
—Tupac Shakur

The Principle of Alternation at Work in Your Life

The principle of alternation will both help you and hinder you as you move forward. It is guaranteed that things will never go exactly as you plan. The fact that all things are in constant motion dictates that the world you are operating in will change as time passes. Nothing will be fixed for the duration of your plan's timeframe. Whether it's in a business or in your personal life, things are constantly changing. This means that your plans will need to change and evolve over time to meet these changing circumstances.

It's like the autopilot on an airplane. The autopilot will plot a course from A to B. As the plane moves along the plotted course, changing winds, unexpected storms, and a host of other things will move the plane off course. In fact, airplanes are off course almost 99 per cent of the time. The autopilot will make thousands of minute course corrections during the journey to bring the plane back onto the plotted course and to its ultimate destination. There is no such thing as a "set-and-forget" plan. Your life's journey, like any other journey, will need a plan that is constantly monitored and adjusted to the inevitable changes in circumstances.

"What we achieve inwardly will change outer reality."
—Plutarch

In developing and monitoring your vision, you must stay focused on what you want to accomplish in your life. Ask yourself this question, "Do I tend to focus more on what I want in life or what I don't want in life?"

It is vital to keep your mind focused on the things you want. If you aren't an optimist by nature, you must work towards becoming one. You must learn to block the things that you don't want in life out of your mind. To put it simply—you can't think about what you don't want without thinking about it. This means that we must control our thoughts. Your mind can only hold one conscious thought at a time. It is your job to make sure that the thoughts you hold in your mind are thoughts that help take you in the direction you want to go.

"Seeing is believing" is an old saying that we have all heard before. It is commonly used to mean that in order for you to believe that something is real, you must see it first. We use this statement in relation to the outside world. When you look around, you see the world outside of yourself—a world that is separate from you. You take it for granted that what you see in that world is real. According to this statement, in order for something to be real, you must be able to see it with your own eyes.

However, there is another old saying, "What you see is what you get." This statement is used in relation to your internal world, the world inside yourself. When you close your eyes, you can see another world, a world completely separate from the outside world, which is not bound by its rules. You see the thoughts, images, and imaginings that run through your mind. This is your internal world. Here you can relive past events or even change their outcomes into what they should have been. In your mind, you can also picture future events and your preferred results. In this world—in your mind's eye—you can "see" the future you want to create. This process is known as visualization.

"The biggest adventure you can ever take
is to live the life of your dreams."
—Oprah Winfrey

Winners in every area of expertise—in sports, the performing arts, business, sales, or any other area of human endeavour—know that visualization works. Visualization is the embodiment of "What you see is what you get."

You can easily prove this to yourself. If you want to make yourself feel bad, simply close your eyes and focus your mind on all the things that have gone wrong for you, all the things you fear might go wrong, all the problems you have had to face, and all the problems you are likely to face in the days ahead. If you focus your mind on doom and gloom, you will create negative, pessimistic thoughts and feelings. If you continue to hold these kinds of thoughts in your mind, they will, slowly but surely, impact the things you say and do. Over time, the actions you take as a result of those negative thoughts will begin to create the very things you dread—with uncanny accuracy—in the real world. Sadly, most people focus the bulk of their mental energy on the things they fear and don't want to have happen to them.

If the above scenario is true, why do some people find it so hard to believe that the opposite could also be true? If you focus your mind on the times you have won, on the times things worked perfectly, on how grateful you are for the good things you have in your life, on how well things are going for you, on how you will perform at your best in the days ahead, and how things will continue going your way, then you will experience a very different mental state. The mental state created by that kind of thinking will result in very different patterns of thought. These more positive thought patterns will result in different actions, which will produce different, more positive results.

How can any of us honestly believe we would not live a happier, healthier, more productive life by focusing on what's going well in life rather than what's going wrong. Sure, it is an absolute certainty that things will go wrong in life. Accept it. Learn from them what you can—and then leave them behind and move on. Don't carry useless negative baggage through life. You write the play, set the stage, and act out the roles for your life, in your mind's eye, every day. You must take great care with the sort of script you're writing for yourself because what you see *is* what you will get."

"Life isn't about finding yourself. Life is about creating yourself."
—George Bernard Shaw

Creating Your Ultimate Vision

It is now time for you to take the next step towards the vision you have for your life. This step is important because it will act as the springboard for what will follow. The more time you devote to getting this part right will make what you need to do in chapter 12 that much simpler.

Continuing with the journey metaphor, this is the part where you need to begin deciding where your point B is. Point A is where you are today, and point B is where you want your journey through life to take you. In chapter 9, you determined the philosophical side of your life. So what you need to do now is to take each of the remaining four areas of your life and decide what each of their point B's look like.

I suggest you use the following process:

Step 1. Take four sheets of paper and write each of the four remaining areas (relational, physical, occupational, and financial) as headings at the top of a page.

Step 2. Begin jotting notes on the relevant page about what your ultimate vision for each of these four areas looks like. Approach this exercise as though you were planning a trip—but weren't exactly sure where you wanted to go yet. A good starting point would be to write down each of the things you would like your preferred destination to offer you. You may need to refer to chapter 3 to make sure that you think about all the elements in each of the four areas. Take your time. This is not a race. This is the journey of your lifetime, and planning it needs to be given your utmost attention.

Step 3. Continue jotting down notes about what you desire from each of the four remaining areas of your life over at least the next week. After you've written something down, take a second and third look at it to see if it still seems right. Look at what you've written down before going to bed so that your mind will continue working on it while you're sleeping. Above all else, do not rush through this exercise. By looking at your list over several days, you will see that some of your initial thinking may change. This is entirely natural.

Step 4. Revisit your values list to ensure that your vision doesn't conflict with any of your core values. There is no use in saying that you want to have, do, or be something that is in direct conflict with your values. Your values are who you are. You must strive to become all that *you* can be—not to become something you aren't.

You may move secondary values up the ladder of importance—maybe even to the level of a core value—but it is far more challenging to add a value that didn't make your initial list, even if that value is needed to remove a conflict between the values you've already chosen and your developing vision. If you truly desire to live a happy, prosperous life, your values must be in harmony with your vision. As you begin looking at the things you think you desire through the prism of the values you hold dear, some things may need to change.

Step 5. Continue adding and deleting from each of your four lists until you feel that your values resonate with each of your desires on all four lists—and that those desires truly represent the ultimate vision you have for your life.

At the completion of this exercise, you will have created a written "picture" of what your ultimate vision looks like. Hold on to these lists because you will need them in chapter 12.

The Vision Process

1. Take four sheets of paper and write each of the four remaining areas (relational, physical, occupational, and financial) as headings at the top of a page.
2. Jot notes on each page about what your ultimate vision for that area of your life looks like.
3. Sleep on it. Revisit your four lists off and on again over the course of at least one week to make sure you still feel the same way.
4. Compare your values list to your vision to ensure that there are no conflicts between who you are (values) and what you want to have, do, and be (vision).
5. Continue adding and deleting until you are sure that your values resonate with all the elements of your ultimate vision.

CHAPTER 11

The Lifeline Graph

"Knowing is not enough; we must apply.
Willing is not enough; we must do."
—Johann von Goethe

At this point, you may wonder whether your vision is realistic. You may wonder whether the point B you've envisioned is achievable. You will recall that I have said over and over that success is simple, but it is not easy. Any change in the direction of your life will present a challenge. How great a challenge—and whether you are willing to get the education you need and put forth the effort required—is a question only you can answer.

People who are able to work through challenges in life and take advantage of the opportunities, know the direction they're heading, the destination they're trying to reach, and the difference between the two.

If you're unsure of the magnitude of the challenge you face to achieve your vision and your own willingness to overcome the obstacles ahead of you, then I suggest using the Lifeline Graph. The Lifeline Graph is a simple visual that will show you the magnitude in the change of direction required to reach your ultimate vision in any of the four areas of your life. You should plot a separate graph for each area of your life you wish to see visually. Simply take the time to plot a graph, or graphs, of where you started, where you are today (point A), and where you want to go (point B) for any or all of the four areas of your life you are concerned about. By plotting all three points on the Lifeline Graph, you will get a sense of the magnitude of the change required in the direction of your relational, occupational, financial, and/or physical progress.

The graph below illustrates the concept of a Lifeline Graph and plots the examples discussed below.

Lifeline Graph

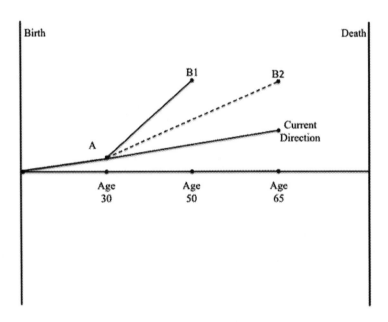

The lifeline graph takes the shape of an elongated capital H. The left leg of this graph indicates the beginning of your life. The right leg of this graph indicates the end of your life. The long line in the middle, connecting the left leg to the right leg, spans the length of your life, about 30,000 days. This line is placed in the middle because it represents the average level of success experienced by people in each of the four areas of life.

To use this simple graph, you will need to plot three points:

1. Where you started out in life
2. Where you are today
3. Where you want to be and when

The Nature-versus-Nurture Debate

The nature-versus-nurture debate will have an impact on where many people place their first dot. This debate has been going on for a very long time. The nature part of the debate concerns your genetic predisposition. In a card game, you'd think of it as the hand you've been dealt. Too often, people say, "I was born this way," or "I've always been like that."

The nurture element is the environment you've grown up in and the type of life you've lived. Some people blame early family circumstances for where they are in life. An element of nature *and* nurture affects virtually everything about you. All five key areas of your life are, to one degree or another, impacted by both nature and nurture. There isn't a lot you can do about your genetic predisposition or your early family life, but—as an adult—you can organize the rest of your life to get the most out of it. You can take control of your life, beginning right now, by making the right choices.

> "If you can't fly, then run; if you can't run, then walk; if you can't walk, then crawl, but whatever you do, you have to keep moving forward."
> —Martin Luther King Jr.

Any good card player will tell you that winning isn't about the cards you've been dealt; it's about how you play those cards. As Kenny Rogers sang in "The Gambler," "Every hand's a winner, and every hand's a loser." The choices you make as you go through life determine whether you turn your nature or nurture hand into a winning hand or not. You can't control where you start in life, but you can definitely control where you finish.

Dot 1: Where You Started Out in Life

The first point is where you believe you were when you started out in life. You will place that dot on the far left axis. If you felt you started out in life at about the average relative to the general population, place a dot where the left vertical axis and the horizontal line meet (see graph above).

For purposes of this example, we've placed a dot at the average (since most people will be at or very near the average). If you felt you started off in life better or worse off than the general population, place a dot above or below the average line to illustrate how much better or worse off you feel you were. As with everything else you do in these exercises, be honest with yourself. The only person you impact by kidding yourself is you.

Dot 2: Where You Are Today

The second point you will plot on the graph is where you are today. This is your point A. There are two elements to plotting this point. The first is your age. Your age is reflected by how far along the horizontal line you are. If the horizontal line consists of about 30,000 days, then simply take your age x 1.217 to calculate your position along that line. This will give you the percentage of the line, from left to right, that you have travelled along. For example, if you're thirty years old, the calculation would be 30 x 1.217 = 36.5 per cent. This means that you have travelled a little over a third of the way along the line.

Once you have determined where you are along the horizontal line, you need to plot where you believe you are relative to the general population. As before, the horizontal line is the average of the general population. You can place a dot at the average line, above it, or below it, depending on where you think you are relative to everyone else.

In the graph above, we have assumed a slightly better than average position for point A because people like you who actively seek to improve their lot in life are typically already in a better place than the general population is.

Dot 3: Where You Want To Be and When You Want To Be There

The final point you will plot also has two elements. This is your point B—the ultimate vision you have for that particular area of your life. The first element in plotting this point is when you want to achieve your ultimate vision for that area of your life. Continuing with the example above, if you wanted to achieve your vision by the time you were fifty, you would do the same age calculation used above (replacing thirty with fifty). The answer would be 60.8 per cent, meaning you would be a bit less than two-thirds of the way along the horizontal line. You would then place this final dot at the point you felt your ultimate vision was in relation to the average of the general population, which is represented by the horizontal line.

For purpose of illustration, we have plotted point B at a position well above the average in the graph above.

Connect the Dots

The final step in using the Lifeline Graph is to connect the three dots you have made on the graph. The line from the first dot to point A shows the trend of your life so far. For clarity on the magnitude of change you are contemplating, extend this line out to the same age point as your point B. This will give you the trend line for your current direction. The line from point A to point B shows the trend needed to be achieved to move from where you are to where you want to be in the desired timeframe. The steeper the change in angle from the trend line for your current direction to your required trend line represents the magnitude of the changes you will be required to make in your life and the size of the challenges ahead.

I have also placed a second point B (dotted line) at sixty-five years of age to illustrate that time, your most valuable asset, can have a significant impact on the magnitude of change required to achieve any given vision. In the example above, by moving our desired end date to age sixty-five from age fifty, we have reduced by almost half the difficulty of achieving our ultimate vision. We've done this by simply giving ourselves some extra time to achieve our vision. Whether you start your new journey earlier in life or give yourself more time to achieve your vision, you can influence the degree of difficulty and the amount of effort required to achieve it.

If you were to use this graph to track the occupational area of your life, for example, you would start at your birth. You may have been born with average intelligence in an average family environment. This would mean that at the time of your birth (the left leg of the graph), you would place a dot at the average line. However, as you went through school, you tended to skip classes and short-change your studies. You put very little effort into your homework, didn't study for tests, and generally tried to get by doing the absolute minimum required. The result of this was that by the time you finished your education, your relative occupational progress had trended downward, finishing below the average line. This means that you would have your work cut out for you getting back over the average line and into the kind of job that will take you where you might want to go. This isn't an insurmountable problem, but remember that a certain amount of effort and education is required to get ahead of the pack in whatever you want to do in life. If you didn't do the work in the past, you'll have to do it in the future. There is no free ride in life.

As in the above example, this graph can be used to track the trends of the quality of your relationships, your level of fitness, your financial position, or the quality of your occupational endeavours. Is your financial lifeline moving towards the financial freedom you desire—or are you just accumulating more debt? Is your physical lifeline moving towards the fit and trim person you want to be—or are you becoming less active and adding a bit more weight every year? Is your relationship lifeline moving towards the happy, engaged relationships you desire—or are you in a routine that sees you continuing to drift away from those you really care about? These are the kinds of things that this simple Lifeline Graph can help you track.

> "Success is not final, failure is not fatal; it is the
> courage to continue that counts."
> —Winston Churchill

The real power of this graph, however, comes into play once you have decided where you want to be in each of the five key areas of your life and when you want to be there. By simply placing a dot at the relative level of success you're striving to achieve and at the time you wish to achieve it, you will be able to regularly determine whether you're trending towards that point and the speed at which you are moving towards it. This allows you to see whether the trend line is pointing in the direction it needs to be pointing or if more needs to be done.

CHAPTER 12

Your Vision Board

"The best way to predict your future is to create it."
—Abraham Lincoln

You must keep the vision you have for your life in your mind at all times. You do this through the constant visualization of that vision. To do this, you must continually reinforce a picture in your mind of the ultimate outcome you desire. Visualization is the process whereby you use your imagination to visualize exactly what your ideal future looks like. What can we do to help this process of visualization? The best tool to help you keep the vision of your ideal life firmly imprinted on your mind is a vision board.

I believe that it's essential for you to create a vision board for yourself. If you genuinely want to achieve the ultimate vision you have for your life, you must have a vision board. As far as your ideal future is concerned, I firmly believe that if you can't see it, you can't be it. A vision board is a narrative and picture of your ultimate vision. It is the simplest and most powerful tool you can create to achieve what you want to achieve in life.

How to Create Your Vision Board

Now is the time to get out the notes that you made while going through the exercise in chapter 10. You will use these notes to help you create your vision board.

Step 1. Start with a large piece of cardboard or poster board. You can buy poster board at just about any stationery store and there are cardboard boxes everywhere.

Step 2. Gather a stack of old magazines, car or travel brochures, real estate booklets, or anything that will likely have pictures that represent the life you're striving to achieve (as described in your notes from chapter 10). If you have access to a colour printer, you can probably find the pictures you'll need on the Internet and simply print them out. This may take a little time, but the payoff will be immense if you do it well.

Step 3. Once you've gathered your source materials, you must begin looking for pictures that represent the vision you have for your life. You must look for pictures that clearly represent how each of the five key areas of your life look. For example, the financial area of your life may be represented by pictures of the kinds of house, cars, holidays, or other things that your future financial position represents.

The occupational part of your life could be represented by pictures of the type of work you would like to be doing, the hobbies you would like to pursue, the new skills you would like to acquire, or anything else that represents what you see yourself doing in your ideal life. The relational side of your life could be shown by using pictures that represent you and your partner and how happy you will be in this new life. You could also use pictures that represent your circle of friends, your family, and the types of activities you will be sharing with them.

The physical part of your life could be represented by pictures showing healthy, active people doing the sorts of things the new you will be doing. The philosophical area of your life may be something as simple as the words themselves shown as a collage of the four to six core values that represent your value system. Your vision board should be a thorough pictorial representation of the life you want to live. Everything you want to have, do, or be should be represented there.

Step 4. Once you have gathered the words and pictures that represent the ultimate vision you have for your life, you must organize them and mount them on your vision board. Start by leaving a space in the centre of the vision board that is sufficient to mount a single sheet of paper with room for the various pictures surrounding it. The pictures should be mounted in such a manner that the words and pictures representing each of the five key areas of your life are clustered in five separate sections. Take time to lay the pictures out on the board before you glue anything in place to make sure that each of the five sections can be properly displayed and are clearly visible. Be sure to leave a space in the centre for one sheet of paper.

Step 5. The work to maximize the value of your vision board isn't over yet because different people learn and relate to the world in different ways. There are three learning styles. Some people are primarily visual and see the world in pictorial form. They literally see pictures in their mind's eye. Other people are primarily auditory. To them, what they hear is more important than what they see. Others are primarily kinaesthetic. For them, it's about how they feel about something more than what they see or hear.

While each of us would be classified primarily as one of these three learning styles, we all have elements of each one. If you're fortunate enough to be a primarily visual learner, then the vision board you've already created will be the most important part of the tool for you. If, however, you're primarily an auditory or kinaesthetic learner, the next step is crucial for maximizing the value of your vision board. For everyone, but particularly for auditory and kinaesthetic learners, the final step is to develop a narrative to go with your vision board.

The narrative should describe, in detail, the type of life the pictures and words in each section represent and the feelings you will experience while you're living that life. The notes you made in chapter 10 will be very useful to you here too. Since the notes are already divided into sections, you can use them as the basis to create a simple narrative of what each section looks like and how you will feel once you've achieved it. It is important to write this narrative as though you have already achieved what the vision board represents. You must write the narrative in the present tense. You should keep this narrative to no more than the remaining space of a standard sheet of paper that was left open in the middle of the vision board. Spend the time to make it descriptive and concise. Once you've got the narrative just how you want it, place it in the centre of your vision board. Your vision board is now complete.

By having both the vision board and the narrative to support it, you will have all the necessary elements for imprinting the ultimate vision for your life into your mind. Since about one-third of the population falls into each of the three learning styles mentioned above—and none of us learn exclusively through one style—it is important to have the vision board and the narrative to go with it.

Step 6. Your vision board needs to be displayed somewhere where you will see it every morning and every evening. On the back of your bathroom or closet door is ideal because you will go there each morning as you get ready for the day and each night as you get ready for bed.

"No one saves us but ourselves. No one can, and no one may.
We ourselves must walk the path."
—Gautama Buddha

How to Use Your Vision Board

Using the vision board is simple. Every morning when you get up and every evening before you go to bed, stand in front of your vision board and read aloud the narrative you have created while looking at the pictures the narrative represents. In the beginning, the process will be a bit challenging because you will need to move your eyes back and forth between the pictures and the narrative. However, once you have been doing it a while, you will find that you will hardly have to look at the narrative at all because it's been virtually memorized.

Once you are able to stand looking at the pictures and recite the narrative verbatim, you will know that you have created a powerful imprint of your ultimate vision in your mind.

The final step in the effective use of your vision board is asking yourself a simple question and answering it. In the morning, ask, "What am I going to do today towards achieving my vision?" In the evening, ask, "What did I do today towards achieving my vision?" The answer to these questions may sometimes be as little as "I told my partner I loved them" (relational) or "I walked around the block" (physical). On an ideal day, you will have done something in each area of your life—and perhaps more than one thing. Obviously, the more steps you take each day within each area of your life, the faster you will move towards your ultimate vision. What you put in (action) is what you get out (result).

The entire visualization process should only take about five minutes. That's five minutes in the morning and five in the evening. That's ten minutes a day to devote to achieving what you want to achieve in life. I don't care how busy you are—everyone can commit ten minutes a day towards this visualization process.

By completing the visualization process, you will see, hear, and feel what it will be like to live the life you chose as your ultimate vision. Twice a day, your mind will fully experience its ultimate destination. Twice a day, it will be reminded where it's going and why it's going there. Ten minutes a day is a very small commitment to make towards living the life you want to live.

Doing this simple exercise every day will not be easy. It will take discipline to continue doing it through good times and bad times, but this discipline separates those who succeed from those who don't.

"There are no gains without pains."
—Benjamin Franklin

This constant visualization of the ultimate vision you have for your life will help keep you focused and moving in the direction you want your life to go. The frequency of your visualization exercises will translate themselves into the speed of motion towards the life that you want to live. In other words, your vision board will help control the motion, speed, and direction your life is taking, and it will harness all that power towards achieving your ultimate vision for life.

Your vision board will not necessarily remain the same for decades. As you move through life, your ultimate vision will change. This is natural. All things change over time. Once something has been achieved, it will invariably be replaced by something else. The beauty of the vision board is that it is not difficult to create—and it is inexpensive to do so.

I can't emphasize it enough, that your vision board is the most important and most powerful tool you have to take control of your life and to begin living the life you want to lead. It is the map that will take you from where you are now to where you want to be in the future. You must hold the vision of what you want your life to look like foremost in your mind, and your vision board will help you do this.

The Vision Board Process

1. Get a large piece of cardboard or poster board.
2. Gather pictures that represent the vision you're striving to achieve for yourself in each area of your life.
3. Mount the pictures by keeping them together in the five separate sections that represent each area of your life. Mount them around a space left in the centre of the poster board that is large enough to hold a single sheet of paper.
4. On a single sheet of paper, write a present tense narrative that describes what each area of your life looks and feels like. Place the sheet of paper in the space provided in the centre of your vision board.

5. Display your vision board somewhere where you will see it every morning and every evening.

6. Every morning, read your narrative aloud while looking at the relevant pictures and ask, "What am I going to do today towards achieving my vision?"

7. Every evening, read your narrative aloud while looking at the relevant pictures and ask, "What did I do today towards achieving my vision?"

CHAPTER 13

Your Milestones

"It's not what you do once in a while; it's what you do
day in and day out that makes the difference."
—Jenny Craig, Weight-Loss Entrepreneur

Life is a journey. By this point in the book, you know your point A
is where you are now, and you're very clear on where your point
B is. Now we must plan how to get from A to B. Just like planning
your driving holiday, you'd get out a map and plot the best
route from A to B. Along that route, you'll probably pass through
a number of towns. You might also have to take different roads
at various junctions along the way.

The end result of this planning exercise is a plan to get from
point A to point B via the best route possible—and you will have a
number of milestones along the way. This becomes your plan for
reaching your eventual destination, or in this case, for achieving
your ultimate vision.

Just like planning a holiday, you need a plan to get you
there, and you need to decide what your milestones will be on
the journey. Instead of towns and road junctions, you will pass
through a number of milestones as you make your way towards
the ultimate vision you have for your life. These milestones are the
interim steps between where you are today and where you want

to be. These milestones are the signposts along your journey that tell you you're still on track and heading in the right direction.

When you begin deciding what your milestones are, you will believe you see, with relative clarity, the short-term road ahead. You will set milestones that tend to assume that everything will go your way. The principle of alternation will intrude to ensure that not all will go as you planned. Just as accidents, detours, and road closures may impact your road trip, things will happen that cause delays or force you to change direction to get where you want to go in life. This doesn't just happen to you. It is a fact in everyone's life. The problem is that some people take it as a sign that the whole process doesn't work and will decide not to continue with it. These people neglect to look at the direction they have moved in the attempt to achieve their ultimate vision and see how that movement is positively impacting their life.

Think of your vision board and the milestones leading towards it like compound interest. If you invest $100 at 7 per cent interest for one year, you end up with $107. If you invest that same $100 for ten years, you end up with $196. You end up with much more than ten times the $7 you made the first year. In fact, you end up with 37 per cent more! That is the power of compound interest. Let's say, however, that you didn't quite achieve your 7 per cent goal in the first year (you only got 6 per cent). In fact, you never achieved your 7 per cent goal and were only ever able to get 6 per cent. After ten years of failure to achieve your 7 per cent goal, you would still end up with more than ten times your original $7 goal! You'd end up with $179, simply by failing to achieve your 7 per cent goal each and every year.

This is why establishing milestones for your journey and keeping a continued focus on reaching them is so important as you strive to move your life in the direction you want it to go. If you had given up after your first year of failing to achieve your

7 per cent goal and took your $100 out of the investment, you never would have "failed" your way to eventual success. If you stop setting milestones for the journey ahead because you didn't achieve them once and didn't want to face the possibility of being disappointed in the future, you will never achieve your ultimate vision. In other words, you will have given up on the journey of your lifetime.

The most important result of having milestones on your journey is not in reaching them; it is the direction that striving to reach them takes you in your daily life. The importance is in the impact that pursuing that milestone has on you. Attempting to reach a milestone will focus your thoughts, drive your actions, and result in movement towards your ultimate vision.

Reaching a particular milestone in a given timeframe gives us all a good feeling, but it is only a very small part of the whole race. As in the old saying, "Success is a journey, not a destination," it is the movement from where you are today towards where you want to be that's the important bit.

"The journey of a thousand miles begins with a single step."
—Lao-Tzu, Chinese Philosopher (circa 550 BC)

Your Milestones

The first step towards developing a plan for your life is to decide upon your first milestone for each of the areas of your life that you want to make changes in. This milestone should be an interim step between where you are now and where you want to be—and be one that you believe you can reach in the next few months. You should only set one milestone for each of the key areas of your life you want to make changes in. Each day, as you use your vision board and ask, "What am I going to do today towards achieving my vision?" and "What did I do today towards achieving my vision?" The answers should be some action you took that leads towards the milestone in each area of your life you wish to make changes in.

You'll reach some of these milestones on schedule—but some you won't. It is even possible that you may never reach some, but take solace from the fact that each milestone that you strive to reach is taking you in the direction you want your life to go. You will be absolutely amazed by how far a decade of "failing" to reach these milestones, on time, will get you!

What I call milestones, many people will call goals. I prefer milestones because they are the markers along the road that you will be travelling on. They're always there, waiting for you to arrive. You may get there quickly—or it may take longer than you expected. Either way, as long as you keep moving towards it, no matter how small the steps, it is almost certain that you will eventually reach it. Depending upon what milestone you are striving to achieve, and which of the key areas of your life it will impact, you will likely end up with a variety of timeframes within which you will measure your progress towards each milestone. As will become obvious to you, different milestones will require different timeframes for their achievement.

It is not my intention here to provide you with a specific goal-setting spreadsheet or a complex goal-setting process to take you through. I believe in the power of simplicity. If you only follow the simple process I outline in this chapter, you will begin making serious progress towards your ultimate vision.

I believe that the milestones should adhere to the SMART system. In 1954, Peter Drucker first suggested using the SMART system to determine if something labelled as a goal, or in my case a milestone, was in fact just that. SMART stands for specific, measurable, action-oriented, realistic, and timely.

Specific means that the milestone itself must leave no room for misunderstanding. Vague milestones are like someone giving you poor directions; while you may be fortunate enough to eventually reach your desired destination, you probably won't get there via the best route or in the time you've allotted to get there. It is just as likely that you will never get there at all. For example, your ultimate vision might be to run a marathon, but your first milestone may be to "walk forty minutes five days a week." Then after a month or so, you may be able to jog for ten minutes and walk for thirty minutes. As your fitness increases, you replace more walk time with jogging time. Eventually, you're jogging for forty minutes. Then you get to a point where you run for ten minutes and jog for thirty, and so on. As you can see, each of these initial milestones is specific, easily understood, and leads towards your ultimate vision.

Measurable means that there must be some objective criteria by which you are able to determine whether the milestone has been achieved. These objective criteria could be as simple as how much time you spent on exercise activities, how much weight you have lost, or how much money you have saved. For example, when setting a fitness milestone, don't say, "Exercise more." Say something *specific*, such as, "Exercise forty minutes five days a week." That way, you can readily *measure* whether you did, in fact, do what you set out to do.

Some types of milestones don't lend themselves to numerical quantification. Relationship milestones, for example, may require the subjective opinion of the person you have the relationship with. However, even in this instance, it would be best if the person whose opinion you are seeking rated your relationship on some sort of agreed scale (e.g. a scale of 1 to 100). That way, you are still able to measure your progress over time.

Action-oriented means that the milestone must require some action on your part. It must require you to do something. The milestone can't be phrased in such a way that you *want* something. It must be that you will *do* something. You may *want* something with all your heart and soul, but if you don't *do* anything about it, nothing will change. Phrase milestones from the standpoint of where you are now and what you will *do* to get where you want to be. These required actions help you re-organize your thinking, increase your discipline, and focus your activity.

Realistic means that you need to set milestones that are progressively more challenging, over time, yet they remain achievable. This means that your milestones should be a series of small steps and not one giant leap. As in the example above, you don't start with running a marathon unless that is a simple step for you to take. You need to set reasonable milestones so that you experience success in order to continue being motivated to establish the next milestone.

Timely means that your milestones must have end dates. Like any other project in life, your milestone must have a deadline. A deadline is necessary because it spurs procrastinators into action. It helps all of us manage time and structure our activities. It is a necessity to keep us focused on what we're trying to achieve and to keep working towards our milestones.

Using the example discussed above, the following would explain how the principles discussed so far in chapters 10, 12, and 13 would work in the real world.

The Vision Board

One of the items in the narrative about the physical section of the vision board is "I will run a marathon by (a date eighteen months from now)." A picture of a marathon runner on the vision board ties in to that part of the narrative.

The First Milestone

Adhering to the SMART principle, the first milestone might be something like "I will walk four kilometres in forty minutes or less, five days a week, for four consecutive weeks by (a date two months from now)."

I will begin my new routine until I do exactly that. If it takes me a few days to get my time down to forty minutes, so be it. Eventually I will get there and do it five days a week for four consecutive weeks.

The Second Milestone

If I've achieved my first milestone after eight weeks, I might need to step it up a bit. The second milestone may be something like "I will jog two kilometres and walk three kilometres by alternating walking and jogging one kilometre each at a time. I will be able to cover the five kilometres in forty minutes or less, and I will do this five days a week for four consecutive weeks by (a date two months from now)."

The first time I do this, it may take forty-five minutes or more, but that's okay because I'm working towards that milestone of forty minutes. Once I've reached it, I will do it five days a week for four consecutive weeks. I believe I should realistically be able do this within the two-month timeframe.

Subsequent Milestones

Each new milestone should build upon the previous one. Each milestone should progressively lead towards the ultimate vision of running a marathon. Between the starting point and running a marathon, there may be a series of ten or more milestones—each moving one step closer to running a marathon. The result is steady progress towards the ultimate vision of running a marathon. This is how you put into practice what we have been discussing so far.

Through the use of your vision board and your milestones in each area of your life, you should try to do at least one thing per day. Each day, do one thing that will move you in the direction you want your life to go. It doesn't need to be huge progress, although it can be, but slow, consistent progress will take you to your desired destination. Life is like a marathon—not a sprint. You need to set a reasonable pace, making consistent progress towards your ultimate vision, and you need to maintain that pace until you get there.

> "You never fail until you stop trying."
> —Albert Einstein

Failure in life is a given. There is no way you will travel through this life and avoid it. The best stock pickers make money on two out of every five shares they buy. Actors will be turned down at twenty-nine out of thirty auditions. Oil companies will strike oil in only one out of every ten wells they drill.

The misses in life will far outnumber the hits in just about everything you can think of. Success is not a function of avoiding failure—but of developing the right responses to its inevitable occurrence. I can guarantee you that you will not achieve the ultimate vision you have for your life without experiencing multiple challenges and setbacks.

Success is the result of discipline combined with appropriate risk-taking. If you travel through life seeking security above all else and avoiding risk at all costs, you will miss the multitude of opportunities that cross your path. Opportunities do not present themselves as safe and secure; they appear as obstacles and challenges. In other words, opportunity presents itself as risk.

Avoidance of risk is the curse of change. To make changes, you must be willing to take chances. All progress is made as a result of change, and change carries risk. Excessive comfort, safety, and security will result in boredom, apathy, mediocrity, and a loss of opportunity. Too often, people look to politicians to provide security and put a floor underneath us, but every structure that starts with a floor finishes with walls and a ceiling. The higher the floor, the lower the ceiling.

> "If you don't make mistakes, you're not
> working on hard enough problems."
> —Frank Wilczek, 2004 Nobel Prize Winner in Physics

Seek change. Embrace risk. Accept failure. Continue on in the face of adversity towards the things you truly want in your life. Joy and fulfilment flow from making progress towards something worthwhile. Don't limit your life to maintaining the status quo and merely hanging on to what you've got.

George Carlin said, "Life is not measured by the number of breaths we take, but by the moments that take our breath away."

The Milestone-Setting Process

1. Decide what your first milestone is in each area of your life. Each milestone should be a small, achievable step towards something on your vision board.
2. Write this milestone down using the SMART system. As in the example used above, "I will walk four kilometres in forty minutes or less, five days a week, for four consecutive weeks by (a date two months from now)."
3. Upon achieving your first milestone, set your second, slightly more challenging milestone, using the same SMART system process.
4. Continue setting and achieving new milestones that slowly, but steadily, move you towards your ultimate vision until you eventually reach it.

Conclusion

"We are what we repeatedly do. Excellence,
then, is not an act but a habit."
—Aristotle

As we go through life, each of us will be faced with the difficulties of changing circumstances. None of us will be exempt from the principle of alternation. It will touch each of our lives. We will all experience success and failure, happiness and heartbreak, good health and illness.

All lives begin at birth and end at death, yet different lives will take very different paths and finish in very different locations. We all have similar destinations in mind. We all seek success—however we may define it. We all seek happiness, good health, financial well-being, and fulfilling relationships. Why do different lives end so differently?

The principle of volition is what takes us to different destinations in life. The starting point for a person's direction in life begins with his or her value system—by the way each of us thinks. The choices we make and the actions we take determine the results we get and make the major difference in where each of us winds up.

Similar circumstances will affect each of us. We will all experience obstacles and challenges in our lives. We will all experience setbacks and times when, despite our best-laid plans and our most diligent efforts, things will just fall apart right before our very eyes. Difficult circumstances are not reserved for any specific individual or group of people. The rich and the poor have health problems. The young and the old have relationship problems. The intelligent and the ignorant experience financial ruin. It is not what happens to us—but rather what we choose to do after it happens—that determines the direction our lives will take.

When things change, we must change. We must remain focused on the vision of our ultimate destinations. We must get out our roadmap, check and see what milestones are still relevant, and find a new way to get where we want to go. The way we think, the choices we make, and the actions we take will always win out over whatever challenges life throws at us.

We must remain willing to work and willing to learn. Through continuous effort and education, we will be prepared to take advantage of the opportunities life puts before us. For just as surely as life sends us challenges, it will also send us opportunities. If we're prepared, we will be able to capitalize on those opportunities. If we're not, they'll just move right on past us because everything in life is in motion at all times.

We must choose right now to go to work on establishing a powerful, personal value system that will help influence, in a positive way, all that we do, think, and decide. If we can succeed in disciplining ourselves to do this, the result will be a dramatic change in the direction of our relationships, our occupations, our finances, our health, and our happiness. In short, we will become truly prosperous and achieve those things we truly value in our lives.

"Happiness is not something ready made.
It comes from your own actions."
—Dalai Lama

When I was young, many parents said, "It isn't whether you win or lose, it's how you play the game." The problem with this statement is that it tends to suggest that winning and playing the game the "right" way are somehow mutually exclusive events. They aren't! What we should be focusing on is winning and doing it the right way. It's not about winning at all costs; it is about playing the game of life with the full intention of winning while playing by the rules.

My dad taught me from a very young age that if you're going to do something, you do your best—or you don't do it at all. There is no nobility in playing at half speed. There is no virtue in striving for mediocrity. Each of us chooses the things we will do in life, and whatever those choices are, we should strive to be the best at them that we can. In each area of our lives—relational, occupational, financial, physical and philosophical—we must commit to being the best we can be. If it's worth doing, it's worth doing well.

The beauty of life is that we can all be winners because we are all striving to achieve different things. Winners are the ones who grow personally and create businesses, families, communities, and countries. Winners drive progress. They are the ones who push for change, develop new things, and innovate. The "next big thing" won't come from the couch potato or the backseat driver—it will come from the person who got up off his or her backside and made it happen.

Winners help others whenever they can because they know there is plenty to go around. There is no maximum quota for wins in any given timeframe. We can all win all the time. By helping others grow, we grow ourselves—and this will make us that much better the next time.

"There are risks and costs to a program of action,
but they are far less than the long-range risks
and costs of comfortable inaction."
—John F. Kennedy

The definition of "know" is to regard as true beyond doubt, to proceed directly with clarity or certainty. If that is the case, then if we truly "knew" something, we could not help but act on it. If you truly knew that eating those chips would make you gain ten kilograms instantly, you wouldn't eat them. If you knew that if you smoked that cigarette, you would die instantly, you wouldn't smoke it.

Since the results of our actions aren't normally instantaneous, we believe we can take the easy path for a while longer and somehow avoid the inevitable outcome. This explains why most people don't make changes in their lives until they find themselves in a truly desperate state.

"Most people would rather suffer the pain
of regret than the pain of change."
—James Rohn

If you are making decisions and doing things that are moving you away from what you truly value in life, you don't really "know" what you say you know. To know and not to do is not to know. We convince ourselves that somehow we will be able to get through life and escape the ultimate results of our actions—and that somehow we will be able to bend the laws of the universe to suit our own personal desires. Not likely. In the end, the odds will win out.

Success and failure in life are not the results of a single action; they are the accumulation of thousands of small decisions and actions over a long period of time. It's not the single bag of chips or cigarette that will kill you—but the many consumed over time. The chips and the cigarette are just examples of the multitude of things we do to sabotage our relationships, our occupations, our finances, and our health every day.

"The brave man is not he who does not feel afraid, but he who conquers fear."
—Nelson Mandela

It is critical that we choose enlightened change rather than frightened change. We must choose to endure the difficulty of change even though it is not easy. If we don't choose the path of enlightened change, we will be left with the pain of regret. We must know the path and walk the path to achieve the things we desire in life. We must choose our paths wisely. True success is determining your path to personal prosperity and then walking it.

It has been a challenge to try to sit down and distil the volumes of information about success that have been written over the years—what it is, what it takes to achieve, how you go about achieving it, and what it means to be successful. After years of trying to make sense of it all, this book is what I believe to be the essence of everything I have learned about success. I hope you walk away from this book with at least three ideas.

First, you must be the one to determine what "success" means to you. The starting place for each of us is deciding exactly what success looks like for us as individuals. There is no single definition of success. Success is what it is to you. Each of us will have a different picture of what success looks like.

Don't buy in to what the media or anyone else tells you success is. It is critical that you decide this for yourself—or it will not be authentic. It will not align with your value system, and you will never achieve it. To be truly successful, you must decide on the right balance for you in the five key areas of your life. You must decide exactly what the relational, occupational, financial, physical, and philosophical parts of your life look like.

> "And in the end, it is not the years in your life
> that count, it's the life in your years."
> —Abraham Lincoln

Second, you must be willing to "pay the price" necessary to become successful. Don't bother designing a life that you are not willing to pay the price to achieve. The "price" is being "willing to work" and "willing to learn." The life you have designed is probably very different from the life you are living at this moment. If it is, you will have to move from where you are now to a very different place. To do this, you must be willing to get whatever education you need to move to this new place, and you must be willing to put in whatever effort is necessary to get to this new life you've designed.

The final critical element of success is that you must be disciplined in your actions. Every day, you will make choices that either move you towards what you want in life or away from it. You know if the choices you are making are consistent with what you say you desire from life or not. You know that going for a walk is better for your health than watching TV. You know that eating a muffin or some chips isn't going to help you lose weight. You know that spending $100 on something you don't really need isn't helping you save money. You know that not spending time with your partner isn't great for your relationship. You know whether you are feeling good about what you're doing with your life. You know whether you're living the life required to get you where you want to go. No one needs to tell you. You know.

The single most important attribute required to achieve whatever it is you desire to achieve in life is self-discipline. If you don't have it, you must develop it. You must have the self-discipline that will be required to get the education and put in the effort that will be needed to achieve the life you've designed for yourself. Without discipline, you will not succeed. Success in life is not easy. If it were easy, everyone would be successful. Achieving success will require you to do a few simple things, consistently—and then to be honest with yourself everyday about whether you're heading in the right direction. It is simple, but it is not easy.

With this book, I hope to have been able to provide you with a simple framework within which to understand life. I hope that you now understand how life works, why it works that way, and what you can do to take better control of it. I believe that, if we are fortunate, sometime during the course of our lives we come upon an insight that starts us on a life-long journey of personal growth and discovery. I hope that this book has fired your imagination about what can be—and who you can become. I hope that you will seek out the things you need to learn in order to become all that you want to become and that you will do whatever you need to do to become the best that you can be. If so, then this book will be all I ever hoped it would be.

Enjoy the Journey!

"Do not let your fire go out, spark by irreplaceable spark in the hopeless swamps of the not-quite, the not-yet, and the not-at-all. Do not let the hero in your soul perish in lonely frustration for the life you deserved and have never been able to reach. The world you desire can be won.
It exists . . . It is real . . . It is possible . . . It is yours."
—Ayn Rand, *Atlas Shrugged*

Printed in the United States
By Bookmasters